NEW GATEWAY TO THE TOEIC® L&R TEST

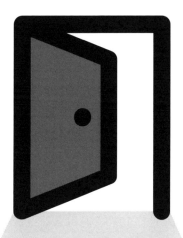

David P. Thompson
Hiroyo Nakagawa
Tomoyasu Miyano

JN084350

KINSEIDO

Kinseido Publishing Co., Ltd.

3-21 Kanda Jimbo-cho, Chiyoda-ku,

Tokyo 101-0051, Japan

First published 2021 by Kinseido Publishing Co., Ltd.

Design: Tomoyuki Adachi (parastyle inc.)

Editorial support: Midoriko Iio (parastyle inc.)

Illustrations: Atsuko Minato

🎧 音声ファイル無料ダウンロード

http://www.kinsei-do.co.jp/download/4126

この教科書で  DL 00 の表示がある箇所の音声は、上記 URL または QR コードにて
無料でダウンロードできます。自習用音声としてご活用ください。

▶ PC からのダウンロードをお勧めします。スマートフォンなどでダウンロードされる場合は、
　ダウンロード前に「**解凍アプリ**」を**インストール**してください。

▶ URL は、**検索ボックスではなくアドレスバー（URL 表示欄）**に入力してください。

▶ お使いのネットワーク環境によっては、ダウンロードできない場合があります。

◎ **CD 00**　左記の表示がある箇所の音声は、教室用 CD（Class Audio CD）に収録されています。

はしがき

TOEIC®（Test of English for International Communication）は、「英語コミュニケーション能力を公平公正に評価する世界共通の基準」です。そして、TOEIC® Listening & Reading Test（以下 TOEIC® L&R）のスコアは、大学入試、単位取得、編入学、さらに就職活動などにおいて、英語力を測るひとつの目安となっています。

本書は、TOEIC® L&Rを受験する際に必要不可欠な知識をトピック別に学ぶとともに、英語の基礎力を養成することを目的としたテキストです。前書 *OPEN THE GATE FOR THE TOEIC® TEST* を新形式のテストに対応させ、改訂しました。本書を通して、授業内外での英語四技能の強化と日常生活に必要な語彙力の増強も可能となります。

前書の最も大きな特長であった文法解説（Grammar Tips）は、本書においても、各章の最初のページに設定し、文法事項のおさらいができるようになっています。また、ひとつひとつの問題に対するヒントや演習問題（Warm Up / Let's Try!）の2段階構成も変わらず、基礎から発展へと段階的に難易度の高い問題に取り組むことができます。

さらに、前書に引き続き、学生になじみのないオフィスでの会話やビジネス文書をわかりやすく理解できるように、イラストや図解を盛り込んでいます。その上、学習者の皆さんが退屈しないように、ペアワーク・グループワークなどを利用して、コミュニカティブな授業展開をはかることも可能となっています。

本書を活用し、TOEIC® L&Rの形式と問題に慣れ、必須項目をマスターするとともに、総合的な英語力の養成に取り組んでください。TOEIC® L&Rの受験を控えた皆さんにも、授業内でご活用される先生方にも、本書が有益なものとなれば幸いです。

皆さんのTOEIC® L&R学習の成功を祈念します。

2021年春　著者

本書の構成と使用法

各章の構成は以下のようになっています。

Grammar Tips
各章で扱う文法項目の基本的な知識をおさらいします。

Part 5 / 6　Check the Grammar
短文穴埋め問題であるPart 5、長文穴埋め問題であるPart 6の問題を学習します。Part 6は Unit 8 / 12のみで扱います。

Part 1　Look at the Pictures
写真描写問題であるPart 1の練習をします。Warm Upでは、スクリプトはテキスト内に表示されていて、一部が穴埋め問題になっています。ディクテーションを行った後、Let's Try!でTOEIC® L&R形式の演習問題に取り組みます。

Part 2 / 3 / 4　Listen to the Questions / Conversations / Short Talks
Warm Upでは、TOEIC® L&R形式の英文［応答問題（Part 2）、会話問題（Part 3）、説明文問題（Part 4）のうちの1種類］を聞きます。スクリプトはテキスト内に表示されていて、一部が穴埋め問題になっています。イラストをヒントにしてディクテーションを行った後、Let's Try!でTOEIC® L&R形式の演習問題に取り組みます。Part 2 / 3 / 4のいずれかを章ごとに扱います。

Part 7　Read the Documents
長文読解問題では、初めにWarm UpでTOEIC® L&Rに頻出するさまざまな文書の形式について図解で学びます。それぞれの文書の特徴を把握した後、Let's Try!で同様のタイプの問題に挑戦し、応用力をつけます。

なお、Unit 1はPre-Test、Unit 15はPost-Testとなっています。学習を始める前の実力診断テストや、実力の伸びを計るための力試しとしてぜひご活用ください。

本書は CheckLink（チェックリンク）対応テキストです。

CheckLink のアイコンが表示されている設問は、CheckLink に対応しています。

CheckLink を使用しなくても従来通りの授業ができますが、特色をご理解いただき、授業活性化のためにぜひご活用ください。

CheckLink の特色について

大掛かりで複雑な従来の e-learning システムとは異なり、CheckLink のシステムは大きな特色として次の3点が挙げられます。

1. これまで行われてきた教科書を使った授業展開に大幅な変化を加えることなく、専門的な知識なしにデジタル学習環境を導入することができる。
2. PC 教室や CALL 教室といった最新の機器が導入された教室に限定されることなく、普通教室を使用した授業でもデジタル学習環境を導入することができる。
3. 授業中での使用に特化し、教師・学習者双方のモチベーション・集中力をアップさせ、授業自体を活性化することができる。

▶ 教科書を使用した授業に「デジタル学習環境」を導入できる

本システムでは、学習者は教科書の CheckLink のアイコンが表示されている設問に PC やスマートフォン、アプリからインターネットを通して解答します。そして教師は、授業中にリアルタイムで解答結果を把握し、正解率などに応じて有効な解説を行うことができるようになっています。教科書自体は従来と何ら変わりはありません。解答の手段として CheckLink を使用しない場合でも、従来通りの教科書として使用して授業を行うことも、もちろん可能です。

▶ 教室環境を選ばない

従来の多機能な e-learning 教材のように学習者側の画面に多くの機能を持たせることはせず、「解答する」ことに機能を特化しました。PC だけでなく、一部タブレット端末やスマートフォン、アプリからの解答も可能です。したがって、PC 教室や CALL 教室といった大掛かりな教室は必要としません。普通教室でも CheckLink を用いた授業が可能です。教師は PC だけでなく、一部タブレット端末やスマートフォンからも解答結果の確認をすることができます。

▶ 授業を活性化するための支援システム

本システムは予習や復習のツールとしてではなく、授業中に活用されることで真価を発揮する仕組みになっています。CheckLink というデジタル学習環境を通じ、教師と学習者双方が授業中に解答状況などの様々な情報を共有することで、学習者はやる気を持って解答し、教師は解答状況に応じて効果的な解説を行う、という好循環を生み出します。CheckLink は、普段の授業をより活力のあるものへと変えていきます。

上記3つの大きな特色以外にも、掲示板などの授業中に活用できる機能を用意しています。従来通りの教科書としても使用はできますが、ぜひ CheckLink の機能をご理解いただき、普段の授業をより活性化されたものにしていくためにご活用ください。

CheckLink の使い方

CheckLinkは、PCや一部のタブレット端末、スマートフォン、アプリを用いて、この教科書にある
CheckLink のアイコン表示のある設問に解答するシステムです。
・初めてCheckLinkを使う場合、以下の要領で**「学習者登録」**と**「教科書登録」**を行います。
・一度登録を済ませれば、あとは毎回**「ログイン画面」**から入るだけです。CheckLinkを使う
　教科書が増えたときだけ、改めて**「教科書登録」**を行ってください。

CheckLink URL

https://checklink.kinsei-do.co.jp/student/

 登録は CheckLink 学習者用
アプリが便利です。ダウン
ロードはこちらから ▶▶▶

▶学習者登録（PC／タブレット／スマートフォンの場合）

①上記URLにアクセスすると、右のページが表示されます。学校名を入力し
　「ログイン画面へ」を選択してください。
　PCの場合は「PC用はこちら」を選択してPC用ページを表示します。同
　様に学校名を入力し「ログイン画面へ」を選択してください。
②ログイン画面が表示されたら**「初めての方はこちら」**を選択し
　「学習者登録画面」に入ります。

③自分の学籍番号、氏名、メールアドレス（学校
　のメールなど**PCメールを推奨**）を入力し、次
　に**任意のパスワード**を8桁以上20桁未満（半
　角英数字）で入力します。なお、学籍番号は
　パスワードとして使用することはできません。
④「パスワード確認」は、❸で入力したパスワー
　ドと同じものを入力します。
⑤最後に「登録」ボタンを選択して登録は完了
　です。次回からは、「ログイン画面」から学籍
　番号とパスワードを入力してログインしてく
　ださい。

▶教科書登録

①ログイン後、メニュー画面から「教科書登録」を選び（PCの場合はその後「新規登録」ボタンを選択）、「教科書登録」画面を開きます。

②教科書と受講する授業を登録します。
教科書の最終ページにある、**教科書固有番号**のシールをはがし、印字された**16桁の数字とアルファベット**を入力します。

③授業を担当される先生から連絡された**11桁の授業ID**を入力します。

④最後に「登録」ボタンを選択して登録は完了です。

⑤実際に使用する際は「教科書一覧」（PCの場合は「教科書選択画面」）の該当する教科書名を選択すると、「問題解答」の画面が表示されます。

▶問題解答

①問題は教科書を見ながら解答します。この教科書の ⟲CheckLink のアイコン表示のある設問に解答できます。

②問題が表示されたら選択肢を選びます。

③表示されている問題に解答した後、「解答」ボタンを選択すると解答が登録されます。

▶CheckLink 推奨環境

PC

推奨 OS
Windows 7, 10 以降
MacOS X 以降

推奨ブラウザ
Internet Explorer 8.0 以上
Firefox 40.0 以上
Google Chrome 50 以上
Safari

携帯電話・スマートフォン
3G 以降の携帯電話（docomo, au, softbank）
iPhone, iPad（iOS9 〜）
Android OS スマートフォン、タブレット

・最新の推奨環境についてはウェブサイトをご確認ください。
・上記の推奨環境を満たしている場合でも、機種によってはご利用いただけない場合もあります。また、
推奨環境は技術動向等により変更される場合があります。

▶CheckLink 開発

CheckLink は奥田裕司 福岡大学教授、正興 IT ソリューション株式会社、株式会社金星堂に
よって共同開発されました。

CheckLink は株式会社金星堂の登録商標です。

CheckLink の使い方に関するお問い合わせは…

正興ITソリューション株式会社　CheckLink 係

e-mail checklink@seiko-denki.co.jp

TOEIC® Listening & Reading Test について

TOEIC® Listening & Reading Test（以下 TOEIC® L&R）は、日常生活やビジネスの場面を中心に、英語で「聞く・読む力」を総合的に測ることを目的としたテストです。合否ではなく、10点〜990点までのスコアで評価されます（リスニングセクションとリーディングセクション、それぞれ5点〜495点）。記述式の問題はなく、全てマークシート方式の選択問題となっています。

TOEIC® L&R の構成

	リスニングセクション（約45分／100問）
Part 1	**写真描写問題：6問** 写真に関する4つの短い英文を聞き、その中から最も写真を適切に描写しているものを選ぶ。英文は印刷されていない。
Part 2	**応答問題：25問** 質問や発言に対する3つの応答を聞き、最も正しい応答を選ぶ。質問・発言・応答は印刷されていない。
Part 3	**会話問題：39問**（1つの会話に3つの設問×13セット） 2人または3人の人物による会話を聞き、その内容に関する3つの設問に答える。会話と図などの情報を関連づけて解答する設問もある。設問と選択肢のみ印刷されている。
Part 4	**説明文問題：30問**（1つの説明文に3つの設問×10セット） 1人の人物による説明文を聞き、その内容に関する3つの設問に答える。説明文と図などの情報を関連づけて解答する設問もある。設問と選択肢のみ印刷されている。
	リーディングセクション（約75分／100問）
Part 5	**短文穴埋め問題：30問** 短い英文の空欄を埋めるのに最も適切な語句を選ぶ。
Part 6	**長文穴埋め問題：16問** 文書を読み、4つの空欄を埋めるのに最も適切な語句または一文を1つ選ぶ。
Part 7	**読解問題：54問**（1つの文書：29問、複数の文書：25問） Eメールや宣伝文などさまざまな文書と設問を読み、最も適切な選択肢を選ぶ。1つの文書の場合は2つ〜4つの設問、複数の文書の場合は5つの設問が出題される。

PROFICIENCY SCALE (TOEIC® L&R スコアとコミュニケーションレベルとの相関表)

レベル	スコア	評価
A	860点以上	Non-native として十分なコミュニケーションができる。
B	730点以上	どんな状況でも適切なコミュニケーションができる素地を備えている。
C	470点以上	日常生活のニーズを充足し、限定された範囲内では業務上のコミュニケーションができる。
D	220点以上	通常会話で最低限のコミュニケーションができる。
E		コミュニケーションができるまで至っていない。

参考資料：一般財団法人 国際ビジネスコミュニケーション協会 公式サイト
http://www.toeic.or.jp/library/toeic_data/toeic/pdf/data/proficiency.pdf

Contents

Unit 1 Pre-Test

Part 1

CheckLink DL 02, 03 CD1-02 CD1-03

Look at the picture and choose the statement that best describes what you see.

1.

(A)   (B)   (C)   (D)

2.

(A)   (B)   (C)   (D)

Part 2

CheckLink DL 04~07 CD1-04 ~ CD1-07

Listen to the question and the three responses, and choose the best response to each question.

3.   (A)   (B)   (C)
4.   (A)   (B)   (C)
5.   (A)   (B)   (C)
6.   (A)   (B)   (C)

Listen to the conversation and choose the best answer to each question.

7. Where does the conversation most likely take place?
   (A) In a coffee shop (C) In a meeting room
   (B) In a clinic (D) At a reception desk

8. Who is the man?
   (A) The woman's supervisor (C) Mr. Swales' client
   (B) The restaurant manager (D) Mr. Carter's subordinate

9. What will the man most likely do next?
   (A) Attend the meeting (C) Fax a document
   (B) Go to the coffee shop (D) Return to his company

Part 4

Listen to the short talk and choose the best answer to each question.

Winchester Park

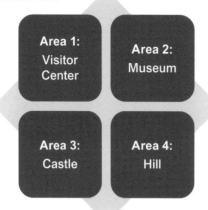

10. Who is the speaker?
    (A) An artist (C) A shop clerk
    (B) A tour guide (D) A tourist

11. What is Winchester Castle known for?

    (A) A famous painting   (C) Its tourist information desk

    (B) A historical story   (D) Its beautiful design

12. Look at the graphic. Which area will the tourists visit right after climbing the hill?

    (A) Area 1   (B) Area 2   (C) Area 3   (D) Area 4

Part 5

ↄCheckLink

Choose the best answer to complete the sentence.

13. When visitors enter the factory, they need to get _____ from the factory manager.

    (A) permissive   (B) permissively   (C) permission   (D) permitted

14. If our project _____ unsuccessful, our bonuses would have been reduced.

    (A) is   (B) are   (C) were   (D) had been

15. The new LED light is both economical _____ eco-friendly.

    (A) and   (B) nor   (C) or   (D) but

16. Mr. and Mrs. Wong had the carpenter repair _____ roof last week.

    (A) they   (B) their   (C) them   (D) theirs

17. The new employee did not remember submitting his _____ expenses to the general affairs.

    (A) administration   (C) identification

    (B) director   (D) transportation

18. _____ the budget was small, the project turned out to be very successful.

    (A) How   (B) If   (C) Although   (D) Unless

19. The company's new CEO has just _____ the conference room.

    (A) enter   (B) enters   (C) entered   (D) entered in

Part 6

Questions 20-23 refer to the following memorandum.

> **To:** All staff members
> **From:** Stephen Jackson, Public Relations Assistant Manager
> **Date:** November 25
> **Subject:** Hudson Company Christmas Party
>
> Dear Staff Members,
>
> We are planning our annual Christmas party to thank all of you once again for your hard work and ---**20.**---.
>
> ---**21.**--- November 20, there was a meeting to plan the details of the party. The party will be held on Friday, December 20 from 6:00 P.M. to 8:00 P.M. in the Banquet Room of the Imperial Hotel in Kyoto. A buffet will be served. We will also have live jazz music.
>
> ---**22.**--- you don't plan to attend the party, please e-mail me by December 5.
>
> ---**23.**---. Please feel free to ask questions regarding this information.
>
> Sincerely,
> Stephen Jackson

20. (A) dedication   (B) dedicate   (C) dedicated   (D) dedicatedly

21. (A) At   (B) Between   (C) In   (D) On

22. (A) Because   (B) If   (C) Despite   (D) Upon

23. (A) The Customer Help Center will support you and answer questions.
    (B) Report your monthly transportation expenses to the General Affairs Department.
    (C) We hope all of you will be able to participate in this event.
    (D) Participants are not allowed to use cell phones once the workshop begins.

Part 7

Questions 24-25 refer to the following advertisement.   CheckLink

---

Tokai City Tour
July 20 – August 31

If you are interested in sightseeing in Tokai City, join our one-day bus tour from Tokai International Airport.

Price: $70 per person / $35 for children under 10
            *Japanese-style lunch is included.
Schedule: 9:00 A.M. – 3:00 P.M.
Route: Airport – Sankaku Temple – Godai Lake – Asian Art Center (lunch) – DEON Shopping Mall – Airport
Option: Electronic translators are available.

Reservations must be made in advance. Please visit Tokai Travel Agency or call 049-5332-1928.

We hope to see you on the Tokai City Tour!

---

24. What is indicated about the Tokai City Tour?
   (A) Participants receive discount shopping coupons.
   (B) It is open only to senior citizens.
   (C) It is available only during a certain period.
   (D) It includes dinner.

25. The phrase "in advance" in paragraph 3, line 1, is closest in meaning to
   (A) out of date
   (B) on time
   (C) behind schedule
   (D) ahead of time

Globe Special Sale
Up to 30% Off
Buy More, Save More!

Founded in Toronto in 1994, Globe is an international brand that offers luxury items such as jewelry, watches, and other fashion items, as well as men's clothes and women's clothes.

For our 20th anniversary, we are having a special sale only for our Globe Club members. For this sale, we are offering delivery within one week.

From July 1 to 10: Buy 1 item, save 10%.

Buy 2 items, save 25%.

Buy 3 items or more, save 30%.

To join our online Globe Club, visit www.globeclub.com.
Sign up now!

From:	dogzenn@mail.com
To:	customerservice@globe.com
Date:	July 13
Subject:	My Order

To whom it may concern,

I ordered three items from your website on July 1. I received the Laure Skirt and the Tower Jacket on order #837 last week. Unfortunately, I have not received the Laure Shirt.

Your ad promised delivery within a week, so the Laure Shirt is now six days late. Please let me know when I can expect it to be delivered.

I look forward to an update on my order. Thank you for your assistance.

Sincerely,
Dona Patel

From: loden@globe.com
To: dogzenn@mail.com
Date: July 14
Subject: Order #837

Dear Ms. Patel,

We are sorry to hear that you have not received your shirt yet. We are currently looking into the cause of the problem with the shipping department. In the meantime, we will send you another Laure Shirt right away.

We would like to express our regrets for this delay. Thank you for calling this matter to our attention.

Sincerely,
Andrew Loden
Customer Service Department

26. In the advertisement, what is suggested about the Globe's products?
    (A) They are only sold in local department stores.
    (B) They are on sale.
    (C) Their quality is only guaranteed for the first year after purchase.
    (D) They will be delivered within six days.

27. What kind of goods did Ms. Patel order?
    (A) Brand name clothing   (C) Jewelry
    (B) Watches   (D) Silk scarves

28. How much of a discount did Ms. Patel receive?
    (A) 10%   (B) 25%   (C) 30%   (D) 35%

29. What is the purpose of the first e-mail?
    (A) To ask about the discount rate
    (B) To complain about a defective product
    (C) To contact the sales department manager
    (D) To find out the status of the order

30. In the second e-mail, the word "regrets" in paragraph 2, line 1, is closest in meaning to
    (A) impatience   (B) gratitude   (C) apology   (D) relief

Unit 2 Daily Life

Grammar Tips 品詞

英語の単語は、働きによっていくつかのグループ（品詞）に分類することができます。ここでは、基本となる品詞（名詞・動詞・形容詞・副詞）の働きについて確認しておきましょう。

This <u>room</u> <u>is</u> <u>very</u> <u>comfortable</u>.（この部屋はとても快適です）
名詞　動詞　副詞　　　形容詞

■**名詞**…………人や物の名前を表す。主語、目的語、補語になる。

■**動詞**…………主語の動作、状態を表す。一般動詞とbe動詞がある。

■**形容詞**………人や物の性質、状態を表す。名詞を修飾したり、補語になったりする。

■**副詞**…………頻度、程度、時などを表す。動詞、形容詞、他の副詞を修飾する。
　　　　　　　また、文頭や文末において文全体を修飾する働きもある。

単語を覚える際には、同じ語から派生した異なる品詞も一緒に覚えると効果的です。例えば、「〜に集中する」という意味の動詞concentrateの場合には、次のように変化します。

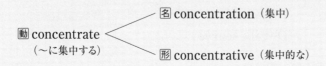
图 concentrate
（〜に集中する）
名 concentration（集中）
形 concentrative（集中的な）

Quiz 空所に適する選択肢を選んで、英文を完成させましょう。　CheckLink

Ms. White _____ on playing the piano for 30 minutes.
（Whiteさんは30分間ピアノを演奏することに集中しました）

(A) concentration
(B) concentrating
(C) concentrated
(D) concentrative

Part 5   Check the Grammar

ココを
Check
Part 5の品詞問題は、**名詞・動詞・形容詞・副詞**の中から空所に適切な品詞を選択するというものです。ですから、**動詞**を覚えるときは**名詞・形容詞・副詞**も同時に覚えてしまいましょう。品詞を見分けるときは**接尾辞**（単語の語尾）に注意すると良いでしょう。

Let's Try!

空所に適する選択肢を選んで、英文を完成させましょう。　　　　　CheckLink

1. The Statue of Liberty is a _____ of the United States.
   (A) symbolism   (B) symbolic   (C) symbolize   (D) symbol
   ▶ a の後ろにくるのは？

2. Some of the discount tickets for Cinema Zone are not _____ anymore.
   (A) avail   (B) avails   (C) availability   (D) available
   ▶ be動詞の後ろにくるのは？「利用できない」という意味の文になるのは？

3. This vacuum cleaner is very _____ because it uses very little electricity.
   (A) economy   (B) economics   (C) economical   (D) economically
   ▶ 電気の使用量が少なければ…？

4. The art gallery near Rainbow Lake is temporarily closed for _____.
   (A) renovation   (B) renovator   (C) to renovate   (D) renovate
   ▶ 前置詞 for の後ろにくるのは？

5. The customer was _____ satisfied with the information provided by Lemon Mall.
   (A) sufficient   (B) sufficiently   (C) sufficiency   (D) suffice
   ▶ 「十分に満足した」という意味になるのは？

Part 1　Look at the Pictures

 写真の内容描写には**現在進行形**（**be動詞＋-ing**）がよく用いられます。問題を解くときには、人物の動作や物の動きなどに注目しましょう。この他にも**写真の場景や場所を表す語句**（on the streetなど）を覚えておく必要があります。

Warm Up

CheckLink　DL 12　CD1-17　CD1-18

音声を聞いて、適切な語を空所に記入しましょう。また、（A）（B）のうち、写真の内容を正しく描写している選択肢を選びましょう。

(A) The man (**i**　　) (**p**　　　　　) the
　　guitar on the street.

(B) Some people are (**p**　　　　　)
　　(**m**　　　　) (**i**　　　　　　).

Let's Try!

CheckLink　DL 13　CD1-19

音声を聞いて、写真の内容を正しく描写している選択肢を選びましょう。

(A)　(B)　(C)　(D)

▶写真の人々の動作は？

10

Part 2 | Listen to the Questions

 ココを
Check

Part 2は、質問文に対して自然な受け答えとなっている応答文を選ぶ問題です。質問文で使われている語句と全く同じものを含んでいる選択肢は誤りであることが多いことに注意しましょう。

Warm Up

CheckLink　DL 14　CD1-20 ～ CD1-23

音声を聞いて、適切な語を空所に記入しましょう。また、(A)(B)(C)のうち、質問の応答として適切な選択肢を選びましょう。

(1.＿＿＿＿＿) are you getting to the (2.＿＿＿＿＿)?

(A) The concert was (3.＿＿＿＿＿).

(B) I'm (4.＿＿＿＿＿), thank you.

(C) Probably by (5.＿＿＿＿＿).

Let's Try!

CheckLink　DL 15 ～ 17　CD1-24 ～ CD1-26

音声を聞いて、質問の応答として適切な選択肢を選びましょう。

1. (A) (B) (C) ▶応答として適切な文脈のものを選ぼう!
2. (A) (B) (C) ▶時制に注意!
3. (A) (B) (C) ▶問われているのが「時」であることに注目する。

Part 7 Read the Documents

 ココを Check

Part 7で非常によく出題されるのがEメールです。Eメールでは、送信者(From)、受信者(To)、送信日(Date)、用件(Subject)などを把握することが大切です。

Warm Up

Eメールを読んで、質問に答えましょう。

🔁 CheckLink

From: Robert Todds \<bobtodds@tnet.uk\>
To: Andrew Carson \<andrew@msit.pcm\>
Date: June 8
Subject: Next Saturday

> 送信者、受信者、送信日、用件などの基本的な情報をここで把握しよう!

Hi Andrew,

——最初の文で用件が明確に伝えられている

Our football team members are having lunch next Saturday. I am not sure if you can make it because you have not come to daily workouts for more than two weeks.

Except for Mr. Tanaka, all members will be there, so I hope you will join us. From tomorrow I'll be in New York for a few days on business, so if you have any questions, please e-mail me, and I'll get back to you as soon as possible.

——受信者にどうしてほしいのか、送信者の意図が読み取れる

I am looking forward to hearing from you.

Regards,

Robert

> Eメールの最後は、結びの挨拶と署名で締めくくられる

Who received the e-mail?

(A) All of the football team members
(B) Andrew
(C) Robert
(D) Mr. Tanaka

12

Let's Try!

Eメールを読んで、質問に答えましょう。

 CheckLink

Questions 1-3 refer to the following e-mail.

From:	jkim@aoe.com
To:	managers@aoe.com
Date:	May 15
Subject:	Agenda for Next Meeting

Dear all,

We are scheduled to have a managers' meeting next Monday. — [1] —. Before you attend the meeting, please read again the agenda I sent you last week. — [2] —. If you have any suggestions or concerns, please e-mail me at jkim@ aoe.com. — [3] —.

If you are not able to come to the meeting, please let me know. — [4] —.

Regards,

Julian Kim
Manager
General Affairs Department

1. Who received the e-mail?
   (A) Clients
   (B) All employees
   (C) All managers
   (D) Julian Kim

2. What is NOT mentioned in the e-mail?
   (A) Contacting Mr. Kim
   (B) Reviewing the agenda
   (C) Giving Mr. Kim suggestions
   (D) Bringing lunch

3. In which of the positions marked [1], [2], [3], and [4] does the following sentence best belong?

   "In addition to the listed topics, we will discuss the budget for our new project."

   (A) [1]   (B) [2]   (C) [3]   (D) [4]

3 Airport

Grammar Tips 時制

動詞の時制は、**現在・過去・未来**の3つに分類することができます。

- ■**現在形**⋯⋯⋯習慣や一般的事実を表す。頻度を表す副詞を伴うことが多い。
- ■**過去形**⋯⋯⋯過去のある時の動作・出来事などを表す。
- ■**未来形**⋯⋯⋯未来の予定、主語の意志を表す。willやbe going toを用いる。

さらに、それぞれの時制には**進行形**と**完了形**が存在します。

- ■**進行形**⋯⋯⋯〈be動詞＋現在分詞〉で特定の時点で進行中の動作を表す。
- ■**完了形**⋯⋯⋯〈have/has/had＋過去分詞〉で、完了、経験、継続などの意味を表す。

例：**I play** tennis with Mr. Joyce.（私はJoyce氏とテニスをします）

	過去	現在	未来
基本形	played	play	will play
進行形〈be動詞＋現在分詞〉	was playing	am playing	will be playing
完了形〈have/has/had＋過去分詞〉	had played	have played	will have played

時制を見分ける際には、副詞や副詞句（last night、next week、nowなど）が重要なポイントとなります。合わせて覚えておきましょう。

Quiz 空所に適する選択肢を選んで、英文を完成させましょう。 ↻CheckLink

Mr. Jacobs _____ a taxi from Terminal 4 only a few minutes ago.
（Jacobs氏はほんの数分前に4番ターミナルからタクシーに乗りました）

    (A) took

    (B) takes

    (C) taking

    (D) has taken

Part 5 Check the Grammar

時制の問題では、**完了形と共に使われることの多い副詞句**に特に注意しましょう。

例：for decades（何十年間）、since last month（先月以来）など

また、特に未来完了形は、「未来のある時までに予想される結果、完了しているであろうこと」を表します。by the end of next week（来週の終わりまでには）、by the time＋主語＋動詞（〜するまでには）といった副詞句も、問題を解くヒントになります。

Let's Try!

空所に適する選択肢を選んで、英文を完成させましょう。　　🔄CheckLink

1. Susan Boyce, the CEO, has _____ Hong Kong once before.
(A) visit　　(B) visiting　　(C) visited　　(D) will visit
▶ 空所の前にhasがあることに注意しよう。

2. Due to the typhoon, the departures of all domestic flights _____ yesterday.
(A) are canceled
(B) was canceled
(C) were canceled
(D) canceled
▶ yesterdayが示す時制は？ 主語は単数、それとも複数？

3. By the end of this year, the East Bridge Airport _____ completed.
(A) was　　(B) is　　(C) has been　　(D) will have been
▶ By the end of this year「今年の終わりまでには」に注意しよう。

4. It did not _____ Roy much time to recover from jet lag.
(A) took　　(B) take　　(C) will take　　(D) taking
▶ did notの後ろにくるのは？

5. Most of the passengers are _____ Flight 356 right now.
(A) boarding　　(B) board　　(C) boarded　　(D) will board
▶ be動詞の後ろにくるのは？

Part 1　Look at the Pictures

ココを
Check

写真の内容描写には現在形あるいは現在進行形が使われますので、**過去時制や未来時制の選択肢が正解になることはありません**。同じ動作を表す表現が用いられていても、問題を解くときには、時制をしっかりと聞き取る必要があります。

Warm Up

CheckLink　DL 18　CD1-27　CD1-28

音声を聞いて、適切な語を空所に記入しましょう。また、(A)(B)のうち、写真の内容を正しく描写している選択肢を選びましょう。

(A) Some people (**h**　　　)
　　(**a**　　　　　)(**b**　　　　　) the
　　airplane.

(B) Passengers (**a**　　)(**c**　　　　　)
　　in at the counter.

Let's Try!

CheckLink　DL 19　CD1-29

音声を聞いて、写真の内容を正しく描写している選択肢を選びましょう。

(A)　(B)　(C)　(D)

▶人物の動作、時制がポイント。

16

Part 3 Listen to the Conversations

 ココを
Check

Part 3は、**日常生活や職場などでの会話問題**です。質問に対して、会話の内容に合っ
ている選択肢を選びましょう。**会話の冒頭にキーとなる表現が登場することが多いた
め、最初の発言を聞き逃さないようにしましょう。**

Warm Up

DL 20 CD1-30 ～ CD1-34

音声を聞いて、会話の空所に適切な語を記入しましょう。

> **M:** Excuse me, I'd like to (1.   ) the departure date of my flight to
> Denver. Are there any seats available tomorrow?
>
> **W:** I'm afraid all of the seats have (2.   ) been <u>booked</u>, sir.
>
> **M:** Could you put me on the (3.   ) list?
>
> **W:** Let me check my computer. Yes, I can, but I don't think there will be any
> chance of getting a seat tomorrow.
>
> **M:** Okay, never mind. I'll use the (4.   ) ticket as I planned. I was
> just wondering if I could do some more (5.   ) with my clients
> by extending my stay. Thank you anyway.

会話中の下線部の語の意味を選びましょう。

 CheckLink

(A) 本   (B) ～を予約する   (C) ～に記入する   (D) 帳簿

Warm Upの会話をもう一度聞いて、質問に答えましょう。

1. Where does the conversation probably take place?
   (A) In an office
   (B) In a bank
   (C) At a theater
   (D) At an airport counter
   ▶前半の会話の内容に注意！

2. What does the man want to do?
   (A) Change his flight schedule
   (B) Cancel his hotel reservation
   (C) Give the woman directions
   (D) Help the woman find an extra seat
   ▶男性の最初の発言から判断できる。

3. Who most likely is the man?
   (A) A flight attendant
   (B) A businessman
   (C) A pilot
   (D) A professor
   ▶後半での男性の発言を聞き取ろう。

Part 7 Read the Documents

 ココを Check Part 7には、**宣伝文やサービスの紹介文**もよく出題されます。どのようなサービスが提供されているのか、具体的な情報を文中から正確に読み取ることが大切です。

Warm Up サービスの紹介文を読んで、質問に答えましょう。 CheckLink

Fire and Rescue at Midway Airport

To ensure the safety of all our passengers, aircrafts and staff, the Fire and Rescue Team at Midway Airport will respond immediately to any emergency.

> 最初に、サービスについての簡単な説明がされている

With over 60 members, the team is constantly ready for any kind of emergency, including:

  — Aircraft accidents — Fires
  — Fire alarms   — First-aid calls
  — Fuel-leaks

> 細かいサービス内容はどのようなものだろうか？

The Fire and Rescue Team at Midway Airport consists of the most experienced and trained members from the Canadian Airport Rescue teams.

For further information, visit our website at www.hh/midway/rescue.

文末には問い合わせ先やウェブサイトの情報が紹介されていることが多い

What is the purpose of the notice?
 (A) To provide information about flight schedules
 (B) To provide information about the airport emergency team
 (C) To notify passengers about website maintenance
 (D) To warn of possible disasters

Let's Try!

宣伝文を読んで、質問に答えましょう。

Questions 1-2 refer to the following advertisement.

Welcome to Star Shuttle

Star Shuttle is the nation's leading airport shuttle service. It provides the most convenient and cost-effective method of airport transportation from your neighborhood or hotel. It helps over nine million passengers get to and from 39 major airports across the United States!

Price: $25 per person / $15 for children under 10
Reservations: Can be made at www.starshuttle.info
Cancellation Policy: We can refund payment if you give us one day's prior notice.

We hope to see you on Star Shuttle.

Notes cost-effective (経済的な) refund (〜を払い戻す) prior notice (事前の連絡)

1. What is NOT indicated about Star Shuttle?
   (A) It allows for cancellations.
   (B) It operates in almost 40 major American cities.
   (C) It costs the same for all passengers.
   (D) It provides an online booking system.

2. The word "leading" in paragraph 1, line 1, is closest in meaning to
   (A) annoying
   (B) difficult
   (C) main
   (D) private

Unit 4 Traffic

Grammar Tips　自動詞・他動詞

動詞は**自動詞**と**他動詞**に分類することができます。

- **自動詞**……… 直後に目的語を取らず、前置詞と共に用いることができる。

  Mr. Jones did not <u>arrive at</u> the office on time.

  （Jones氏は、定刻に事務所へ到着しませんでした）

- **他動詞**……… 直後に目的語を取り、前置詞を必要としない。

  Ms. Jones <u>discussed</u> the document with her co-worker.

  （Jonesさんは同僚とその書類について話し合いました）

他動詞と間違えやすい自動詞	自動詞と間違えやすい他動詞
agree with ~（～に同意する） object to ~（～に反対する） refer to ~（～に言及する）	approach ~（～に近づく） enter ~（～に入る） reach ~（～に到着する）

動詞の多くは自動詞にも他動詞にも用いられますが、**同じ単語でも意味が異なる場合**があります。

例：consult（自相談する、他～を調べる）

　　sell（自売れる、他～を売る）

Vegetables <u>are selling</u> well at this store.（この店で野菜はよく売れています）

Most grocery stores in this town <u>sell</u> everything.

（この町のほとんどの食料品店ではなんでも売っています）

Quiz 空所に適する選択肢を選んで、英文を完成させましょう。　　　　**⟲ CheckLink**

Mr. Johns has just _____ at Central Station.

（Johns氏はCentral駅に到着したばかりです）

    (A) arrive

    (B) arrived

    (C) reached

    (D) reach

Part 5 Check the Grammar

ココを
Check

自動詞・他動詞の問題において間違えやすいのが、riseとraise、lieとlayの区別です。それぞれの意味と動詞の活用形に特に注意しましょう。

rise – rose – risen　　　自上がる　　　lie – lay – lain　　自横たわる

raise – raised – raised　他〜を上げる　　lay – laid – laid　他〜を置く、横たえる

Let's Try!

空所に適する選択肢を選んで、英文を完成させましょう。　　　　　　　　CheckLink

1. As of April 1, all of the train fares in Block City will _____.
   (A) rise　　　(B) rose　　　(C) raise　　　(D) raised
   ▶主語は何だろうか？

2. All of the city's bus drivers are seriously _____ tomorrow's strike.
   (A) discussed　　　(B) discussing about　　　(C) talking about　　　(D) talking
   ▶「〜について話している」という意味を表すのは？

3. A lot of people have just _____ the theater on the 3rd floor of the Community Library.
   (A) entered　　　(B) enter　　　(C) enters　　　(D) entered in
   ▶空所の前の完了の助動詞haveに注意！

4. We _____ the Safe Driving seminar held at the community center in front of Central Station.
   (A) were attended　　　(B) attended　　　(C) attended at　　　(D) attended in
   ▶主語は人か物か。目的語にも注意！

5. Mr. Hershey _____ down on the bed right after he came home because he was very tired.
   (A) lie　　　(B) lay　　　(C) laid　　　(D) lain
   ▶空所の後ろの前置詞に注意！ 時制は？

Part 1   Look at the Pictures

 ココを
Check
人物の動作に関するほとんどの問題には、**1人だけが写っている写真**が使用されています。このような場合、全ての選択肢の主語が同じで、**動作のみが異なる動詞によって描写されている**パターンが多いことを覚えておきましょう。

Warm Up

 CheckLink   DL 23   CD1-41   CD1-42

音声を聞いて、適切な語を空所に記入しましょう。また、(A)(B)のうち、写真の内容を正しく描写している選択肢を選びましょう。

(A) The man with the (**h**   ) is
   (**b**   ) on the (**p**   ).

(B) The man with the (**s**   )
   is (**r**   ) (**a**   ).

Let's Try!

 CheckLink   DL 24   CD1-43

音声を聞いて、写真の内容を正しく描写している選択肢を選びましょう。

(A)   (B)   (C)   (D)

▶女性と乗物の位置関係は?

Part 4　Listen to the Short Talks

ココを
Check
Part 4には、トーク、アナウンス、スピーチ、メッセージ、広告、ニュースなどの説明文が出題されます。Part 3と同様に、問題用紙には設問と選択肢のみが印刷されています。**説明文が放送される前に設問と選択肢を先に読み、説明文の内容を推測しておく**ことが大切です。

Warm Up

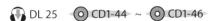
DL 25　　CD1-44 ～ CD1-46

音声を聞いて、トークの空所に適切な語を記入しましょう。

Thank you for listening to Jay's Traffic Report. Today, we're (1.　　　　　　) to have a heavy traffic <u>jam</u> from about 7 A.M. to 10 A.M. on Riverside Avenue because of a visit by popular British football player, Ben Rogers. All of the roads around Riverside Avenue will be (2.　　　　　　) closed. If you usually drive, we recommend that you use (3.　　　　　　) transportation such as the bus or the subway instead. Upon (4.　　　　　　), Rogers is going to join the Sports Festival near City Hall. For (5.　　　　　) information, stay tuned to 63.5 FM, Jay's Traffic Report. Thank you.

トーク中の下線部の語の意味を選びましょう。

CheckLink

(A) ［果物の］ジャム　　　(B) 交通渋滞　　　(C) ～を詰まらせる　　　(D) ～を妨害する

Let's Try!

 CheckLink   DL 26   DL 27   CD1-47 ~ CD1-49   CD1-50

Warm Upのトークをもう一度聞いて、質問に答えましょう。

1. What is the talk mainly about?
   (A) A singer's concert
   (B) A sports game
   (C) Road construction
   (D) Traffic congestion
   ▶トークの出だしと締めくくりの言葉に注意！

2. Who is Ben Rogers?
   (A) A broadcaster
   (B) A journalist
   (C) A radio announcer
   (D) An athlete
   ▶Ben Rogersの名前と共に紹介される職業について注意して聞き取ろう。

3. What does the speaker suggest listeners do?
   (A) Take a longer vacation
   (B) Use alternative means of transportation
   (C) Purchase a new vehicle
   (D) Watch football games on television
   ▶話し手は何を提案している？

Part 7 Read the Documents

ココを
Check

Part 7には**告知文**もよく出題されます。告知文には、**交通情報や公共施設に関する連絡**（断水や停電）などがあります。**日時、場所、注意事項**などに気をつけて読み取ることが大切です。

Warm Up　告知文を読んで、質問に答えましょう。

CheckLink

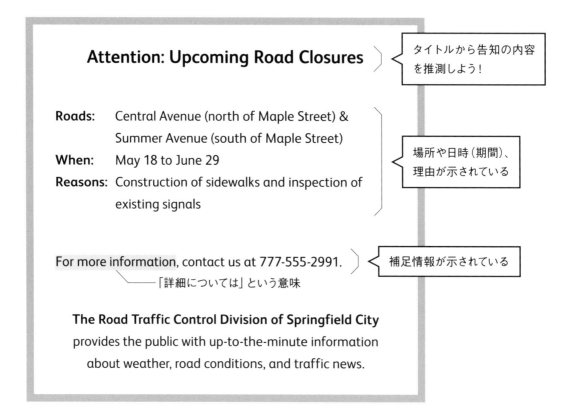

Attention: Upcoming Road Closures

> タイトルから告知の内容を推測しよう！

Roads: Central Avenue (north of Maple Street) & Summer Avenue (south of Maple Street)
When: May 18 to June 29
Reasons: Construction of sidewalks and inspection of existing signals

> 場所や日時（期間）、理由が示されている

For more information, contact us at 777-555-2991.
└── 「詳細については」という意味

> 補足情報が示されている

The Road Traffic Control Division of Springfield City
provides the public with up-to-the-minute information about weather, road conditions, and traffic news.

What is the purpose of the notification?
   (A) To announce a new security policy
   (B) To prevent forest fires
   (C) To inform people of updated road conditions
   (D) To warn about sudden weather changes

告知文を読んで、質問に答えましょう。   CheckLink

Questions 1-2 refer to the following notification.

Boston Technical College
Bike Lane & Pedestrian Bridge Closures

All bike lanes and east/west pedestrian bridges on campus will be closed.

When: November 13, 7 A.M. to December 12, 6 A.M.
Reason: Repairs at the power plant on campus

- The use of underground tunnels is required.
- Fire lanes by the East Building will also be inaccessible on weekdays during this period.
- Internet access on campus will not be affected.

We sincerely apologize for any inconvenience.

Ian Crookes
Security Department Manager

Notes pedestrian (歩行者) inaccessible (アクセスできない)

1. Approximately how long will the situation continue?
   (A) One week
   (B) Two weeks
   (C) One month
   (D) Two months

2. According to the notification, what will be available during the closures?
   (A) Online usage
   (B) Cycling paths
   (C) Fire lanes
   (D) Pedestrian bridges

Grammar Tips 主語と動詞の一致

TOEICでは、問題文の主語に対して適切な動詞の形を選択する、主語と動詞の一致の問題がよく出題されます。主語が1人または1つの事物を表すときは単数形、2人または2つ以上の場合は複数形です。対応する主語によって、動詞の活用が変化します。例えば、単数形の主語のときには単数形に対応した動詞、複数形の主語のときには複数形に対応した動詞を選ぶ必要があります。

Mr. Smith **is** always complaining about his work.
(Smith氏はいつも仕事について不満を言っています)

Mr. Smith and his assistant **are** having lunch at the Italian restaurant.
(Smith氏と彼の助手は今イタリア料理店で昼食をとっています)

以下のように、主語の後に修飾語句が入り、主語と動詞が離れている場合には特に注意が必要です。

The man working with volunteers over there **is** my former supervisor.
(あそこでボランティアと働いている男性は私の以前の上司です)

以下は特にTOEICでよく出題されます。

■〈A number of＋複数名詞〉「いくつかの～、多くの～」
A large number of participants in the contest **were** excited.
(多くのコンテストの参加者は興奮していました)

■〈The number of＋複数名詞〉「～の数」
The number of participants in the contest **was** unexpectedly high.
(コンテストの参加者の数は予想外に多かったです)

Quiz 空所に適する選択肢を選んで、英文を完成させましょう。 CheckLink

The number of visitors to Seoul last April _____ more than 10,000.
(ソウルを訪れた旅行者の数は、昨年の4月で1万人以上でした)

(A) is　　(B) was　　(C) are　　(D) were

Part 5 Check the Grammar

ココを Check 以下の語が主語の場合、**単数扱い**となりますので気をつけましょう。

anyone、anything、everyone、everything、no one、nothing、someone、something

また、〈each/every +単数名詞〉も単数扱いとなります。

Let's Try!

空所に適する選択肢を選んで、英文を完成させましょう。　　　　　🔄CheckLink

1. Currently, the number of employees in King Hotel _____ decreasing because of budget cuts.

   (A) is　　(B) are　　(C) was　　(D) were

   ▶ the number of ~が主語であることに注意！

2. Each guest _____ required to fill out the form when they check in.

   (A) have　　(B) has　　(C) are　　(D) is

   ▶ requiredの意味は？ 文頭にあるEachにも注目。

3. All members of City Sport facility _____ able to use its swimming pool every day.

   (A) has been　　(B) have been　　(C) is　　(D) are

   ▶ 主語は単数か複数か？

4. Mr. and Mrs. Lee _____ visit their grandchildren in a few weeks.

   (A) are going to　　(B) had　　(C) has　　(D) is going to

   ▶ 主語は単数か複数か？ 時制は？

5. A large number of visitors _____ accessing the Internet, so the connection is not available now.

   (A) was　　(B) were　　(C) is　　(D) are

   ▶ 主語は何？ 時制は？

Part 1 Look at the Pictures

ココを
Check

人物が描写されている写真の場合、特に**身体的な特徴や服装**（髪の長さ、帽子、サングラスなど）、**姿勢や様子**、**持ち物**などに注意しましょう。

Warm Up

CheckLink DL 28 CD1-51 CD1-52

音声を聞いて、適切な語を空所に記入しましょう。また、(A) (B) のうち、写真の内容を正しく描写している選択肢を選びましょう。

(A) Both women (**a**   ) (**s**   ) in the lobby.

(B) The woman with long hair (**i**   ) (**t**   ) to the receptionist at the counter.

Let's Try!

CheckLink DL 29 CD1-53

音声を聞いて、写真の内容を正しく描写している選択肢を選びましょう。

(A)   (B)   (C)   (D)

▶写真の女性の持ち物は？

Part 2   Listen to the Questions

 ココを
Check

Part 2 で最もよく出題されるのが WH 疑問文です。What（何が／を）、Who（誰が／を）、When（いつ）、Where（どこで）、Why（どうして）、How（どのようにして）をしっかり聞き取り、質問文の内容を把握することが必要です。時には遠回しな応答が正解となる場合もあるので、正確に話し手の意図を理解し、正しい答えを選びましょう。

Warm Up

 CheckLink   DL 30   CD1-54 ~ CD1-57

音声を聞いて、適切な語を空所に記入しましょう。また、(A)(B)(C) のうち、質問の応答として適切な選択肢を選びましょう。

(¹.   ) is the
nearest (².   ) stop?

(A) At (³.   )
o'clock.

(B) Let me check it on
your (⁴.   ).

(C) With his
(⁵.   ).

Let's Try!

CheckLink   DL 31 ~ 33   CD1-58 ~ CD1-60

音声を聞いて、質問の応答として適切な選択肢を選びましょう。

1. (A) (B) (C)   ▶ Where を聞き取れれば、すぐにわかるはず。
2. (A) (B) (C)   ▶ cafeteria という語に惑わされないように注意！
3. (A) (B) (C)   ▶ 理由を適切に答えている選択肢を選ぼう。

ココを
Check

Part 7にはアンケート形式になった文書も出題されます。まずは、どのようなサービスについてのアンケートなのかを理解した上で、**具体的な評価内容や客の要望を読み取る**ことが大切です。

Warm Up　アンケートを読んで、質問に答えましょう。　⟳ CheckLink

🌴 **Oasis Inn**

Guest Comments

Thank you for choosing Oasis Inn for your trip. We would appreciate your comments in order to make future stays with us more enjoyable.

Guest Name　*Bella Noel*　　**Room Number**　1145

	Excellent	Good	Adequate	Fair	Poor
Overall	☐	☐	☐	✔	☐
Guest Rooms	☐	☐	☐	☐	✔
Bar & Restaurants	☐	✔	☐	☐	☐
Gym	☐	✔	☐	☐	☐

評価項目とチェックがついている位置に注目しよう！

Comments

I was not satisfied with your room. I booked a room with ocean view, yet I was not given such a room. I requested a change of rooms right away, but the hotel was fully booked.

コメント欄を見れば、より具体的な評価（問題点や改善点など）がわかる

What is Bella complaining about?

(A) The housekeeping

(B) The food

(C) A room

(D) A swimming pool

Let's Try!

アンケートを読んで、質問に答えましょう。

 CheckLink

Questions 1-2 refer to the following questionnaire.

Jenny's Indian Restaurant Customer Feedback Form

Jenny Khan began this Indian Restaurant 10 years ago. Now it is time to evaluate our performance and services. With your feedback, we will make necessary changes to improve the restaurant environment, the quality of the food, and our services.

Guest name(s)   *Anne and Hanna*

	Excellent	Good	Average	Poor
Quality of food	✓	☐	☐	☐
Customer service	✓	☐	☐	☐
Price	☐	✓	☐	☐
Cleanliness	✓	☐	☐	☐
Menu selection	✓	☐	☐	☐

Comments

We would like to express our satisfaction with your restaurant. We have been coming for lunch for several years. Although you increased the prices last month, the overall services and quality of food are very good. We intend to continue coming here.

Note   evaluate（〜を評価する）

1. According to the form, what is implied about the restaurant?
   (A) The restaurant has just been opened.
   (B) The restaurant is planning to keep things as they are.
   (C) The customers are able to eat Italian food.
   (D) The customers are mostly content with this restaurant.

2. Who most likely is Jenny Khan?
   (A) A tourist
   (B) The first owner
   (C) The first customer
   (D) A part-time staff member

6 Bank

Grammar Tips 受動態

主語が動作を行う場合、「〜する」という意味の**能動態**、主語が動作を受ける場合は「〜される」という意味の**受動態**（受け身）を使います。受動態は〈be動詞＋過去分詞（＋by 行為者)〉で表します。

能動態の目的語を主語にすると、受動態に書き換えることができます。

能動態：The clerk <u>usually calculates</u> all of the receipts.
　　　　（その店員は通常全ての伝票を計算しています）

受動態：All of the receipts <u>are usually calculated</u> by the clerk.
　　　　（全ての伝票は通常その店員によって計算されています）

以下のような場合もありますので注意しましょう。

助動詞を含む場合：The document <u>should be reviewed</u> by the manager.
　　　　（その書類は部長によって見直されるべきです）

完了形の場合：The document <u>has already been reviewed</u> by the manager.
　　　　（その書類はすでに部長によって見直されました）

進行形の場合：The document <u>is being reviewed</u> by the manager.
　　　　（その書類は部長によって見直されているところです）

Quiz 空所に適する選択肢を選んで、英文を完成させましょう。　　　　　ＣＣheckLink

The ATM is regularly _____ early in the morning.
（ATMは早朝に定期的に検査されます）

    (A) inspect
    (B) inspects
    (C) has inspected
    (D) inspected

Part 5   Check the Grammar

ココを Check

受動態の問題では、**特定の前置詞およびto不定詞と共に使われる表現**に注意しましょう。

be entitled to ～（～の資格がある）   be replaced by ～（～に取って代わられる）
be nominated for ～（～の候補になる）   be scheduled to *do*（～する予定である）
be engaged in ～（～に専念する）   be supposed to *do*（～することになっている）

Let's Try!

空所に適する選択肢を選んで、英文を完成させましょう。   ⟲ CheckLink

1. The postage for postcards will ＿＿＿＿ next year.

   (A) raise   (B) be raised   (C) is raising   (D) raises

   ▶主語は動作を行っている？ 助動詞の後の動詞の形は？

2. The new operation system has just ＿＿＿＿.

   (A) installing   (B) installed   (C) be installed   (D) been installed

   ▶問題文は能動態、それとも受動態？ 完了の助動詞hasに注意！

3. The employee ＿＿＿＿ to work a little longer tomorrow.

   (A) is scheduled   (B) schedule   (C) being scheduled   (D) scheduled

   ▶「～する予定である」という意味を表すのは？

4. Earth Bank ＿＿＿＿ a monthly luncheon meeting on the second Friday of every month.

   (A) was held   (B) hold   (C) holds   (D) is held

   ▶「銀行が会議を開く」という意味であるなら、問題文は受動態、それとも能動態？

5. The online banking system of Sky Blue Bank was ＿＿＿＿ several years ago.

   (A) implemented

   (B) been implemented

   (C) implement

   (D) implementing

   ▶be動詞wasの後ろにくるのは？ 主語にも注意！

ココを
Check

1人の人物が大きく写っている写真では、その**人物の動作や行為に特に注意して聞き取**りましょう。写真からはっきり判断できないことは誤りとなります。

Warm Up

CheckLink　DL 34　CD1-61　CD1-62

音声を聞いて、適切な語を空所に記入しましょう。また、(A)(B)のうち、写真の内容を正しく描写している選択肢を選びましょう。

(A) The woman (**i**　　) (**t**　　　) some mail from the mailbox.

(B) The woman (**i**　　) (**s**　　　) the (**e**　　　　).

Let's Try!

CheckLink　DL 35　CD1-63

音声を聞いて、写真の内容を正しく描写している選択肢を選びましょう。

(A)　(B)　(C)　(D)

▶写真の人物の動作と向いている方向は？

Part 3 Listen to the Conversations

 ココを
Check

Part 3には、**何かのトラブルやその解決法についての会話**がよく出題されます。キーワードを頼りに、**人物の関係や会話が行われている状況を推測**することが大切です。

Warm Up

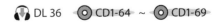 DL 36 ◎ CD1-64 ~ ◎ CD1-69

音声を聞いて、会話の空所に適切な語を記入しましょう。

> **W:** Oh, no. I can't believe it! It isn't working again.
>
> **M1:** Hi, Michelle. What's up?
>
> **W:** My (1.) has some problems. Could you look at it, please?
>
> **M1:** I'm afraid I'm too busy at the (2.). I'm supposed to meet my clients in 10 minutes and then I have to revise some reports. Hey, Steve, can you possibly help her?
>
> **M2:** No problem. Let me take a look. Hmm, I guess we need someone else to (3.) it. Why don't you ask an expert to look at it?
>
> **W:** Thank you for your (4.). I'll call the (5.) department and ask for someone to <u>check it out</u>.

会話中の下線部の語句の意味を選びましょう。

 CheckLink

(A) ［ホテルなどから］チェックアウトする　　(C) ［レジ係が］精算をする

(B) ［図書館などから］～を借りる　　(D) ［機械などを］点検する

Warm Upの会話をもう一度聞いて、質問に答えましょう。

1. What is the woman's problem?
   (A) Her computer is not running well.
   (B) Her printer is out of ink.
   (C) Her colleagues are too demanding.
   (D) Her clients are late.
   ▶会話中でproblemsと言っている部分に注意!

2. Why does Steve say, "No problem"?
   (A) To confirm an appointment
   (B) To promote an advertisement
   (C) To suggest a solution
   (D) To show willingness to do something
   ▶直前の男性の質問から判断しよう。

3. What is the woman going to do next?
   (A) Consult her manager
   (B) Fix the copy machine
   (C) Phone a technician
   (D) Rewrite an invoice
   ▶女性が会話の最後に言ったことは?

Part 7　Read the Documents

ココを
Check

Part 7には**新聞記事や雑誌記事**も出題されることが多く、合併や企業の活動に関する内容がよく扱われます。新聞記事では、**見出しや冒頭部分から記事の概要を読み取る**ことが重要です。

Warm Up　記事を読んで、質問に答えましょう。　　🔗CheckLink

Unexpected Merger Causes Loss of Faith in Banks

見出しから、記事の内容を推測しよう！

新聞記事では、冒頭に要点がまとめられている

Greece's Finance Ministry has just reported a surprising merger. The merger between the Bank of Athena and the European Bank was necessary in order to keep both banks afloat. The Bank of Athena's customers were shocked to find out that their bank had suddenly merged with a rival bank.

The merger has been completed, but in this recession no one knows how this merger will solve the ongoing financial crisis.

Linda Jolieとは？

A financial consultant, Linda Jolie, criticized the merger because some customers have lost faith in their banks.

どのような見解が述べられているだろうか

Note　afloat（破綻せずに）

According to Linda Jolie, what was the result of the merger?

(A) Bankruptcy

(B) The loss of customers' trust

(C) The resignation of top management

(D) Deeper economic problems

Questions 1-2 refer to the following article.

Swiss Union Bank Eyes Asian Merger

At a press conference on August 10, a spokesperson from Swiss Union Bank announced that a merger with the Bank of Tokyo may be possible next year.

Swiss Bank was a large financial company in Zurich in the 1990s. It merged with European Union Bank in 2005 and became Swiss Union Bank, the second largest bank in the world.

The spokesperson from Swiss Union Bank stated that they need to acquire a number of banks in Asian countries, such as South Korea and China, in addition to Japan. However, no firm decisions have yet been made.

Note press conference (記者会見)

1. What is the subject of the article?
   (A) A conflict between two countries
   (B) Housing information
   (C) A proposed merger
   (D) The unemployment rate

2. What was the former name of Swiss Union Bank?
   (A) Swiss Bank
   (B) Bank of Tokyo
   (C) European Bank
   (D) Union Bank of Switzerland

Unit 7 Office

Grammar Tips 不定詞・動名詞

不定詞（**to＋動詞の原形**）は、文中で名詞（〜すること）、形容詞（〜するための…）、副詞（〜のために）の働きをします。

The assistant decided <u>to leave</u> early today.
（助手は今日早く出発することを決めました）

I want something <u>to drink</u>.（私は何か飲み物がほしいです）

We worked hard <u>to increase</u> our sales.
（私達は売上を増加させるために一生懸命働きました）

動名詞（**-ing**）は、動詞の性質と名詞の役割の両方を持っています。文の主語、目的語、補語、前置詞の目的語になることができます。

We have just <u>finished cleaning</u> our office.
（私達はちょうど事務所の掃除を終えたところです）

動詞には、不定詞・動名詞のどちらが後に続くかによって意味が大きく異なる場合がありますので注意しましょう。

例	不定詞	動名詞
forget	〜するのを忘れる	〜したのを忘れる
remember	忘れずに〜する	〜したのを覚えている
stop	〜するために休止する	〜するのをやめる

We remember seeing the new secretary at the party.
（私達は新しい秘書にパーティで会ったのを覚えています）

Please remember to e-mail me. （私に忘れずにEメールを送ってください）

Quiz 空所に適する選択肢を選んで、英文を完成させましょう。 **C**heckLink

Please do not forget ＿＿＿＿ your assistant when you arrive at the branch in Chicago.
（シカゴ支社に着いたら助手に電話するのを忘れないでください）

(A) calling (B) call (C) to call (D) called

Part 5 Check the Grammar

 ココを
Check

目的語に不定詞のみを取る動詞、動名詞のみを取る動詞は以下の通りです。
不定詞のみを取る動詞：agree、decide、expect、hesitate、hope、intend、offer、refuse、wantなど
動名詞のみを取る動詞：admit、avoid、consider、deny、discontinue、enjoy、finish、include、keep、mind、miss、postpone、quit、suggestなど

Let's Try!

空所に適する選択肢を選んで、英文を完成させましょう。　　　　　ℭ CheckLink

1. _____ the agenda is one of the essential tasks.
(A) Complete　　(B) Completing　　(C) Completion　　(D) Completed
▶主語を作るためには何が必要？

2. The marketing team decided _____ the sales promotion campaign when the company had to reduce the workforce.
(A) cancel　　(B) to cancel　　(C) canceling　　(D) to canceling
▶動詞 decide は目的語に何を取る？

3. Some of the project members seriously considered _____ their proposals.
(A) withdrawn
(B) to withdraw
(C) withdrawing
(D) will withdraw
▶動詞 consider は目的語に何を取る？

4. The new receptionist hesitated _____ customers on her first day of work.
(A) to help　　(B) helpful　　(C) helping　　(D) help
▶動詞 hesitate の後ろにくるのは？

5. Please note that we offered _____ all details of the new policy to our employees.
(A) to explain　　(B) explain　　(C) explaining　　(D) explained
▶動詞 offer の後ろにくるのは？

Part 1　Look at the Pictures

ココを
Check

場所に関する写真では、焦点があてられているものが何であるかを予め予測することが大切です。〈There is/are＋主語〉で「～がいる／ある」という意味を表します。また、場所を表す前置詞句が選択肢に含まれている場合は、人物や物の位置関係にも注意しましょう。

Warm Up

CheckLink　DL 39　CD1-77　CD1-78

音声を聞いて、適切な語を空所に記入しましょう。また、(A)(B)のうち、写真の内容を正しく描写している選択肢を選びましょう。

(A) The books (**a**　　) all (**p**　　　　)
　　(**u**　　) on the shelf.

(B) There (**a**　　) several (**d**　　　　　)
　　and a laptop on the table.

Let's Try!

CheckLink　DL 40　CD1-79

音声を聞いて、写真の内容を正しく描写している選択肢を選びましょう。

(A)　(B)　(C)　(D)

▶人物の視線と物の位置に注目。

Part 4 Listen to the Short Talks

ココを
Check
Part 4には、ビジネスに特化したスピーチがよく出題されます。例えば、講演、セミナー、レセプションなどがあります。注意すべき点は、目的、対象となる聴衆、スピーチのテーマなど、話し手が伝えたい内容です。スピーチの流れを把握して、問題を解きましょう。

Warm Up

🎧 DL 41   ◉ CD1-80 ～ ◉ CD1-82

音声を聞いて、スピーチの空所に適切な語を記入しましょう。

> Thank you for coming to Dr. Anna Olson's ($^{1.}$)
> party tonight. She <u>contributed to</u> the Institute of Tribal Art
> for over three decades. She taught primitive art history and
> also exhibited her own ($^{2.}$) in our community
> centers. In fact, she received ($^{3.}$) on several
> occasions for her work. Now she's planning to be involved in
> the downtown redesign project at the ($^{4.}$) of the
> mayor. We're very proud of her. Please give Dr. Olson a big
> round of ($^{5.}$).

スピーチ中の下線部の語句の意味を選びましょう。

 CheckLink

(A) ～に反した　　(B) ～に貢献した　　(C) ～に従った　　(D) ～に配布した

44

Let's Try!

CheckLink DL 42 DL 43 CD1-83 ~ CD1-85 CD1-86

Warm Upのスピーチをもう一度聞いて、質問に答えましょう。

1. What is the purpose of the speech?
   (A) To start a farewell reception
   (B) To give a student an award
   (C) To encourage primitive art
   (D) To announce a city planning project
   ▶話し手の発言の出だしがポイント。

2. Where most likely is the speaker?
   (A) In a banquet hall
   (B) In a fitness center
   (C) In the mayor's office
   (D) In a hotel lobby
   ▶冒頭の表現に注意しよう。

3. What is Dr. Olson going to do in the future?
   (A) Establish a business training school
   (B) Manage a new branch office
   (C) Take part in city planning
   (D) Work as a freelance journalist
   ▶スピーチの後半で述べられていることは？

ココを
Check

メッセージチェーンでは、誰が何を述べているかに注意しましょう。その上で、チャットの中でほのめかされている内容について、文脈から読み取るようにしてください。

Warm Up メッセージチェーンを読んで、質問に答えましょう。　　　　🔄 CheckLink

Emma Woods (1:00 P.M.)
Hi Olivia. Did you check out the e-mail about the year-end party?

> Emmaが Oliviaに連絡をした目的を考えてみよう

Olivia Valentine (1:01 P.M.)
No, not yet. Why?

Emma Woods (1:02 P.M.)
Bryan just called me. It looks like he needs your help. Could you call him?

Olivia Valentine (1:05 P.M.)
Sure. I'm at my client's office now, so I'll call him later.

> Oliviaはこの後、何をするつもりか想像してみよう

At 1:05 P.M., what does Ms. Valentine mean when she writes, "Sure"?

(A) She will call Bryan.
(B) She will e-mail Emma.
(C) Emma will call Bryan.
(D) The party will be canceled.

Let's Try!　メッセージチェーンを読んで、質問に答えましょう。　CheckLink

Questions 1-2 refer to the following text-message chain.

> **Takao Yoshida (9:30 A.M.)**
> Can you do me a favor? I need someone to review my PowerPoint slides for an upcoming sales presentation.

> **Tony Jensen (9:34 A.M.)**
> Of course. When is the presentation?

> **Takao Yoshida (9:36 A.M.)**
> Tomorrow afternoon. Can I stop by your office this afternoon?

> **Tony Jensen (9:38 A.M.)**
> Well, I have an appointment with a client at 1:00, but anytime from 2:00 is fine.

> **Takao Yoshida (9:40 A.M.)**
> Thanks. I'll be there at 2:00, then.

1. What is being discussed?
   (A) Planning a business trip
   (B) Interviewing candidates
   (C) Launching a sales promotion
   (D) Reviewing a presentation

2. At 9:34 A.M., what does Mr. Jensen mean when he writes, "Of course"?
   (A) He will attend the sales meeting.
   (B) He will be away on business.
   (C) He will help Mr. Yoshida.
   (D) He will meet his client tomorrow.

Grammar Tips 分詞

分詞には、**現在分詞**(**-ing**)と**過去分詞**(**-ed**)があります。現在分詞は動作の進行、能動を表し、「〜している」という意味になります。過去分詞は受動(受け身)や完了を表し、「〜された」、「〜してしまった」という意味になります。どちらも形容詞のように働き、名詞を修飾します。

現在分詞：The employee writing the reports is Mr. Smith.
(報告書を書いている従業員はSmith氏です)

過去分詞：This projector made by the Gold Company is user-friendly.
(Gold社によって作られたこのプロジェクターは使いやすいです)

分詞が動詞と接続詞の2つの働きをし、副詞のように主節を修飾する構文を**分詞構文**といいます。分詞構文で、時・理由・条件・譲歩・付帯状況などの意味を表すことができます。

Adjusting the microphone, the speaker began his presentation.
(マイクを調整して、発表者はプレゼンテーションを始めました)

Knowing that the boss would soon arrive, all of the staff started preparing for the meeting.
(上司がまもなく到着すると知り、スタッフ全員が会議の準備を始めました)

Quiz ▶ 空所に適する選択肢を選んで、英文を完成させましょう。　　CheckLink

The government official _____ by the Prime Minister did not arrive on time.
(首相に招待された官僚は、定刻に到着しませんでした)

   (A) invite

   (B) inviting

   (C) invited

   (D) invitation

Part 6 Check the Grammar

 ココを Check
Part 6は、空所の前後に注意すれば適切な選択肢を選ぶことができます。以下は、Part 6によく出てくる**分詞を使った慣用表現**です。

frankly speaking（率直に言えば） weather permitting（天気が良ければ）
generally speaking（一般的に言えば） judging from ~（～から判断すると）
strictly speaking（厳密に言えば）

Let's Try! 空所に適する選択肢を選んで、英文を完成させましょう。 CheckLink

Questions 1-4 refer to the following article.

According to the results of a questionnaire ---**1.**--- to businesspeople under the age of 30, most of them are ---**2.**--- with their assigned work. ---**3.**---. Judging from their answers, they seem to feel that they are productive, unless their managers often interfere in their ---**4.**---.

1. (A) distributing (B) distribute (C) distributed (D) to distribute
▶「～に配布された」という表現を考えてみよう。

2. (A) satisfactory (B) satisfied (C) satisfying (D) satisfaction
▶「～に満足している」という表現を考えてみよう。

3. (A) They ended contracts with several clients because of the budget cut this year.
(B) Approximately 30 new employees are expected to be hired on August 25.
(C) There might be people of different ages working together.
(D) The results also showed that working independently improves their efficiency.
▶アンケート結果を述べている前後の文にうまくつながる適切な文は？

4. (A) projects (B) resources (C) tokens (D) utilities
▶会社員が取り組むことは何か考えてみよう。

Part 1 Look at the Pictures

 ココを Check

ここでは、**2人以上の人物を描写している写真**について学習しましょう。複数の人物が写っている場合、写真から読み取れる**人物の関係性**（受付と来訪者、店員と客など）に注目することがポイントです。

Warm Up

 CheckLink　DL 44　CD2-02　CD2-03

音声を聞いて、適切な語を空所に記入しましょう。また、(A)(B)のうち、写真の内容を正しく描写している選択肢を選びましょう。

(A) The speaker is (**h** 　　　)
　　(**t** 　　　) the audience.

(B) The audience is (**p** 　　　)
　　(**a** 　　　) to the speaker.

Let's Try!

CheckLink　DL 45　CD2-04

音声を聞いて、写真の内容を正しく描写している選択肢を選びましょう。

(A)　(B)　(C)　(D)

▶ 2人は何をしている？

Part 2 Listen to the Questions

 ココを Check
Part 2では、Yes/No疑問文も出題されます。注意したいのがAren't you ～?や Don't you ～?などの**否定疑問文**です。解答の際には、実際に尋ねられている内容が 何であるか、文中の疑問詞（when/where/whatなど）や動詞を意識して聞き取るよう 心がけましょう。

Warm Up

 CheckLink DL 46 CD2-05 ～ CD2-08

音声を聞いて、適切な語を空所に記入しましょう。また、(A)(B)(C) のうち、質問の応答として適 切な選択肢を選びましょう。

(¹.   ) you know
(².   ) the meeting begins?

(A) No, he (³.   ).

(B) Maybe at
(⁴.   ).

(C) Yes, one month
(⁵.   ).

Let's Try!

CheckLink DL 47～49 CD2-09 ～ CD2-11

音声を聞いて、質問の応答として適切な選択肢を選びましょう。

1. (A) (B) (C) ▶ Do you think 以降に注意して聞こう。

2. (A) (B) (C) ▶「何を見る必要があるのか」に注意！

3. (A) (B) (C) ▶ 質問文の時制に対応するものを選ぼう。

ココを Check　Part 7では複数の関連文書を読んで設問に答える**Multiple Passages**の問題も出題されます。この章では、**社内メモとそれに対する問い合わせのEメール**を通して、2つの文書に関する問題形式を学びましょう。

Warm Up　社内メモとそれに対する問い合わせのEメールを読んで、質問に答えましょう。　**↻ CheckLink**

MEMORANDUM

To:　　　All staff
From:　　Diane Houston, Assistant Sales Manager
Subject:　Sales Presentations

> 社内メモでは、宛先がいつも個人とは限らないので、しっかり確認しよう！

As you know, we will release new models of electronic dictionaries in a few months.

Before we start our sales campaign, our team would like to explain the products to everyone. We ask you to attend our upcoming sales presentations.

Mr. Suzuki in the sales department and Ms. Chong in the manufacturing department will make 30-minute presentations.

The presentations will be held at 10:00 A.M. on October 10 in Conference Room A. Registration is not required. If you need more information, feel free to contact me at dhouston@patmail.com.

> ——多くの場合、メモの内容についての問い合わせ先が最後に明記されている

I hope to see you there.

Diane

To:	dhouston@patmail.com
From:	jcostello@patmail.com
Date:	October 1
Subject:	Upcoming Sales Presentations

Dear Diane,

Thank you for letting us know about the presentations. Unfortunately, I won't be able to be there because I have an appointment with a client. It looks like some of my staff won't be available either.

> 最初の段落に社内メモへの返信がまとめられている

―― どのような依頼内容が続いているだろうか？

I wonder if you could record the presentations so that everyone can get the information we need about the new products.

I am looking forward to hearing from you soon.

Best regards,

Jason Costello
Advertising Manager

---

1. What is the main subject of the memo?

(A) Budget cuts

(B) A job advertisement

(C) Diane Houston

(D) Presentations

2. Why did Mr. Costello send the e-mail?

(A) To suggest recording the presentations for absent staff

(B) To inquire about the new products

(C) To provide a social event with clients

(D) To register in advance

Questions 1-5 refer to the following memorandum and e-mail.

MEMORANDUM

To: All senior staff
From: William Kettle, Advertising Manager
Subject: Friday's Meeting

The next meeting will be held at 11:00 A.M. this Friday in Room 101 in the World Tower.

We have invited well-known designers from Paris. Those designers will advise us on our new project. We will also be reviewing proposals for advertising campaigns from our new staff.

We would like to have senior staff there to share ideas with our new staff. We are looking forward to everyone meeting each other.

William

To: wkettle@styles.com
From: akimura@styles.com
Date: November 5
Subject: Next Meeting

Hi William,

Thank you for reminding us of the meeting.

As for the proposals from our new staff, it would be helpful if we could look at them in advance. Attached is a list of senior staff in my department who are attending the meeting. Could you send us the proposals?

Sincerely,

Amy Kimura
Senior Manager
Marketing Department

1. What is indicated about Friday's meeting?
   (A) It will take place in Paris.
   (B) It will start at 11:00 A.M.
   (C) Only senior staff will attend the meeting.
   (D) All of the products have sold out.

2. Who will be invited from abroad?
   (A) Designers
   (B) Senior staff
   (C) New employees
   (D) The advertising manager

3. What is most likely true about the new staff?
   (A) They are going to meet designers in Paris.
   (B) They will arrange the upcoming event without any help.
   (C) They attended the meeting.
   (D) They are involved in making proposals.

4. What is Mr. Kettle asked to do?
   (A) To revise the proposals by himself
   (B) To provide information to some of the participants
   (C) To give comments on the agenda
   (D) To announce an upcoming conference

5. What is NOT true about Ms. Kimura?
   (A) She will probably attend the meeting.
   (B) She hopes to see the proposals before the meeting.
   (C) She works in the same department as Mr. Kettle.
   (D) She sent a list to Mr. Kettle.

9 Employment

Grammar Tips 可算名詞・不可算名詞

名詞とは「人や物の名前を表す語」のことです。名詞には**可算名詞**（数えられる名詞）と**不可算名詞**（数えられない名詞）があります。可算名詞は、単数の場合はa/anがつき、複数の場合は複数形になります。不可算名詞はa/anがつかず、複数形にはなりません。動詞の形に注意しましょう。

可算名詞：The <u>employees</u> are working at the <u>desks</u>.
（従業員達は机に向かって仕事をしています）

不可算名詞：We need <u>advice</u> from a financial expert.
（私達は金融専門家からの忠告を必要としています）

この章で扱うトピックで頻出する可算名詞と不可算名詞を覚えておきましょう。

可算名詞	applicant（応募者）、desk（机）、employee（従業員）、machine（機械）、worker（労働者）
不可算名詞	advice（忠告）、air（空気）、furniture（家具）、information（情報）、luggage／baggage（荷物）、money（お金）、news（ニュース）、water（水）、weather（天候）

■可算名詞を修飾するときには、a fewやmanyなどを用います。
I'll be there in <u>a few minutes</u>.（あと2、3分でそこに着きます）

■不可算名詞を修飾するときには、a littleやa piece of、muchなどを用います。
There is <u>a piece of information</u> about a rival company.
（ライバル社について情報がわずかにあります）

Quiz 空所に適する選択肢を選んで、英文を完成させましょう。 ⟲CheckLink

We need a piece of _____ in the new office.
（私達は新しい事務所に家具が必要です）

    (A) many furnitures   (B) a furniture   (C) furnitures   (D) furniture

Part 5 Check the Grammar

ココを Check

集合名詞とは、同じ種類のものが集まった1つの集合体を表している名詞のことを示します。その集合体の個々に重点を置く場合は複数扱い、集合体全体を単体とみなす場合は単数扱いになります。

例：audience（聴衆）、family（家族）、committee（委員会）、public（大衆）

複数扱いにしかならない集合名詞には、people（人々）やpolice（警察）などがあります。

Let's Try!

空所に適する選択肢を選んで、英文を完成させましょう。　CheckLink

1. The White family _____ all excited about their new lives when they moved to a new town last year.
   (A) is　(B) are　(C) was　(D) were
   ▶主語は個々を指している？

2. People _____ concerns about the current unemployment rate.
   (A) is　(B) are　(C) has　(D) have
   ▶peopleは集合名詞。名詞concerns（心配事）の前に置くのに適切な意味となる動詞は？

3. Mr. Whitman got _____ from today's guest speaker after the lecture.
   (A) an advice
   (B) a piece of advice
   (C) advices
   (D) many advices
   ▶不可算名詞adviceを修飾するものは？

4. The committee _____ supposed to have several gatherings next month.
   (A) be　(B) were　(C) is　(D) was
   ▶問題文の時制は？

5. Only _____ people have finished the registration at the reception.
   (A) few　(B) a few　(C) little　(D) a little
   ▶主語peopleは単数扱い？ 複数扱い？

ココを
Check
写真問題では、**似た音をもつ単語にも気をつけなければなりません**。例えば、fold（折りたたむ）とhold（持つ）、walk（歩く）とwork（働く）などです。

Warm Up

CheckLink   DL 50   CD2-12   CD2-13

音声を聞いて、適切な語を空所に記入しましょう。また、(A)(B)のうち、写真の内容を正しく描写している選択肢を選びましょう。

(A) Two women (**a**) (**f**)
their reports.

(B) Two women (**a**) (**h**)
a meeting.

Let's Try!

CheckLink   DL 51   CD2-14

音声を聞いて、写真の内容を正しく描写している選択肢を選びましょう。

(A)   (B)   (C)   (D)

▶写真の人物が手にしているものは？

Part 3 Listen to the Conversations

 ココを
Check
Part 3の会話のどこにヒントがあるのでしょうか。会話がA→B→A→Bと進んでいく場合、Aの最初の発言で会話の要点が推測できます。そして、**会話が進むほど、解答につながるヒントが隠されています**。会話の終盤には話し手が今後行うことについて述べている部分がいくつかあります。最後まで集中して聞きましょう。

Warm Up

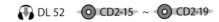 🎧 DL 52　◉ CD2-15　~　◉ CD2-19

音声を聞いて、会話の空所に適切な語を記入しましょう。

> **W:** Have you started recruiting for the Manufacturing Department yet?
>
> **M:** Yeah, we posted a (¹.　　　　　　) ad on our website last week. Actually, we've received a large number of (².　　　　　　) so far.
>
> **W:** Are there any competent (³.　　　　　　)?
>
> **M:** Yes, there're a lot. Some have practical (⁴.　　　　　　) experience; others have professional knowledge in fields such as engineering and marketing analysis.
>
> **W:** It seems you'll be <u>conducting</u> (⁵.　　　　　　) very soon.

会話中の下線部の語の意味を選びましょう。　　　Ｃ CheckLink

(A) 振る舞う　　(B) ~を伝導する　　(C) ~を行う　　(D) ~を指揮する

Warm Upの会話をもう一度聞いて、質問に答えましょう。

1. What is the main subject of the conversation?
   (A) Setting up a website
   (B) Hiring new staff
   (C) Laying off employees
   (D) A pay increase
   ▶会話の冒頭に注意！

2. In which department does the man most likely work?
   (A) Human resources
   (B) Sales
   (C) Quality control
   (D) Manufacturing
   ▶男性の最初の発言から推測できる。

3. How does the man respond to the information?
   (A) He feels funny.
   (B) He feels indifferent.
   (C) He feels disappointed.
   (D) He feels satisfied.
   ▶男性の二度目の発言に注意！

Part 7 Read the Documents

 ココを
Check

Part 7には**求人広告**もよく出題されます。**職種や応募条件、連絡方法**などの情報を正確に読み取ることが大切です。

Warm Up 広告を読んで、質問に答えましょう。 CheckLink

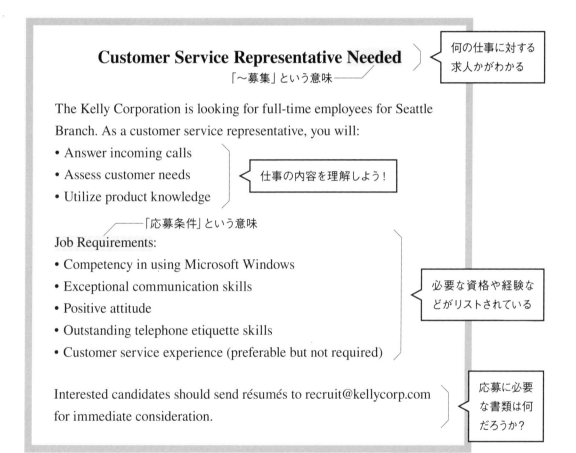

What is the purpose of the advertisement?

    (A) To announce a job position

    (B) To evaluate staff progress

    (C) To inspire creativity

    (D) To schedule a meeting with clients

Let's Try!

Questions 1-2 refer to the following advertisement.

Part-Time French Teacher Needed

We have a part-time teaching job for a beginners' French class available at Alberta French Language School. Below are the minimum qualifications required for the job:
- Bachelor's degree in French
- Proficiency in both spoken and written French
- Two years of teaching experience

A full job description can be seen on our website at http://albertafrenchschool.com.

To apply for the position, send a cover letter, résumé, and two recommendations by e-mail to bonnie.brunswick@gnet.com.

Bonnie Brunswick
Director of Human Resources
Alberta French Language School

Note qualification (資格)

1. What is NOT a requirement of the position?
   (A) A university degree
   (B) French language skills
   (C) Previous teaching experience
   (D) Computer skills

2. The word "recommendations" in paragraph 2, line 1, is closest in meaning to
   (A) instructions
   (B) suggestions
   (C) references
   (D) proposals

Grammar Tips 代名詞

代名詞は、対象となる名詞の代わりに用いられます。例えば、第三者について話す場合、名前の代わりにhe（彼）やshe（彼女）を用いることができます。

A: Have you heard from <u>Mr. Lee</u> lately?（Lee 氏から最近連絡がありましたか）
B: Yes, **he** e-mailed me yesterday.（はい。彼は昨日私にEメールをくれました）

すでに述べられた人や物を表すさまざまな代名詞を表にまとめました。覚えておきましょう。

人称			人称代名詞			所有代名詞	再帰代名詞
			主格	所有格	目的格		
単数	1人称		I	my	me	mine	myself
	2人称		you	your	you	yours	yourself
	3人称	男性	he	his	him	his	himself
		女性	she	her	her	hers	herself
		物	it	its	it	—	itself
複数	1人称		we	our	us	ours	ourselves
	2人称		you	your	you	yours	yourselves
	3人称		they	their	them	theirs	themselves

Quiz 空所に適する選択肢を選んで、英文を完成させましょう。 ⚡CheckLink

Fresh vegetables need to be put in the fridge after _____ are delivered.
（新鮮な野菜は配達された後、冷蔵庫で保管する必要があります）

 (A) they
 (B) it
 (C) them
 (D) their

Part 5 Check the Grammar

ココを Check

Part 5の代名詞の問題では、特に**itとoneの使い分け**に注意しましょう。

I lost my pencil. I'm looking for <u>it</u>. (= my pencil)

➡ なくした鉛筆そのものを探している

I lost my pencil. I need to buy <u>one</u>. (= a pencil)

➡ 鉛筆をなくしたので、代わりの鉛筆が必要である

Let's Try!

空所に適する選択肢を選んで、英文を完成させましょう。　⟲**CheckLink**

1. Since her secondhand car occasionally had engine trouble, Ms. Yamada wanted to buy a new _____.
   (A) it　　(B) its　　(C) one　　(D) ones
   ▶「代わりのもの (車)」という意味を表すのは？

2. Mr. Wilson is famous for _____ amazing inventions.
   (A) he　　(B) him　　(C) his　　(D) himself
   ▶「誰の」発明？

3. A software company made great profits from _____ new products.
   (A) it　　(B) its　　(C) it's　　(D) they
   ▶所有の意味を表し、後ろの名詞を修飾する人称代名詞は？

4. Most computer users are happy that _____ will be able to purchase updated products soon.
   (A) they　　(B) their　　(C) theirs　　(D) them
   ▶that節の主語になることに注意！

5. The director requested that _____ subordinates cancel the meeting.
   (A) he　　(B) his　　(C) they　　(D) their
   ▶所有の意味を表し、後ろの名詞を修飾する人称代名詞は？

Part 1　Look at the Pictures

ココを
Check
人物を主語とし、現在進行形（be動詞 + -ing）を用いてその人の動作を表す文はPart 1でよく出題されます。しかし、必ずしも全ての問題がそうではありません。**物を主語とし、受動態を使って物の状態が表されている場合**もあります。

Warm Up

音声を聞いて、適切な語を空所に記入しましょう。また、(A)(B)のうち、写真の内容を正しく描写している選択肢を選びましょう。

(A) Some devices (**a**　　) (**b**　　　　)
　　(**u**　　　) at the plant.

(B) Some products (**a**　　) (**u**　　　　) the
　　wooden table.

Let's Try!

音声を聞いて、写真の内容を正しく描写している選択肢を選びましょう。

(A)　(B)　(C)　(D)
▶どのような場面だろうか？

Part 4 Listen to the Short Talks

 ココを
Check

Part 4はビジネスに関するスピーチやトークが多く出題されます。ここでは、新入社員を対象とした研修のトークを聞いて、空所に適切な語を記入しましょう。

Warm Up

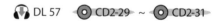 DL 57　CD2-29 ～ CD2-31

音声を聞いて、トークの空所に適切な語を記入しましょう。

Hi, new employees. Welcome to Bridge Beer Company. I'm Christina Henderson, the sales manager. Let me talk about today's schedule. First, we'd like you to learn about our products. Next, Linda Byron, the assistant sales manager, will show you a film about our company history. Then Peter Raymond, the (1.   ) manager, will take you on a factory tour. A free lunch will be (2.   ) at 12:30 in the cafeteria. OK, let's start with the recent sales <u>performance</u> of our new beer. Due to (3.   ) cold weather, sales did not (4.   ) to 20,000 cases as forecasted for the first two months. However, our new TV commercials started in the following month and we received a (5.   ) response. You can see the sales dramatically rising this month. Now Paul Gardner, our product manager, will explain more about our new beer.

トーク中の下線部の語の意味を選びましょう。

 CheckLink

(A) 演技　　(B) 業績　　(C) 上演　　(D) 実行

Let's Try!

↻CheckLink 🎧 DL 58 🎧 DL 59 ◉ CD2-32 ~ ◉ CD2-34 ◉ CD2-35

Warm Upのトークをもう一度聞いて、質問に答えましょう。

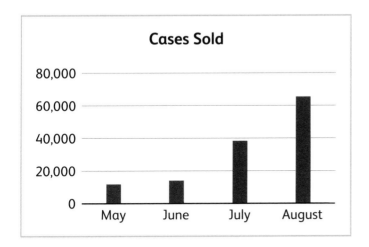

1. Look at the graphic. When did the company launch its TV commercials?

(A) In May

(B) In June

(C) In July

(D) In August

▶トークで「宣伝」という意味を表す言葉に注意しよう。

2. Who is supposed to talk in detail about the new product?

(A) Christina Henderson

(B) Linda Byron

(C) Peter Raymond

(D) Paul Gardner

▶放送の前に選択肢を先読みして、トークを聞いてみよう。

3. What will be offered to the listeners?

(A) A half-day tour ticket

(B) A DVD of the factory's history

(C) A sample of a new product

(D) A complimentary meal

▶質問文のoffered「提供される」の類似語はトークの中でどれであるか考えてみよう。

ココを
Check

Part 7では、欠陥製品のリコール（回収）を知らせる通知文も出題されます。製品について の説明や欠陥の詳細、問題点、対処法などの情報に注意して読み取りましょう。

Warm Up

通知文を読んで、質問に答えましょう。

 CheckLink

Dawn Ltd.
Product Recall: LED Night-Light 105

何の製品のリコールな のかを把握しよう

We have identified a quality concern with LED Night-Light 105. It may go out unexpectedly. The light was made without an internal fuse. In certain situations this may cause other components of the light to fail.

製品の問題点に ついて具体的に 説明されている

To avoid any possible problems, we have decided to recall the product as a precautionary measure.

購入者はどうするべき？

Please stop using the product and return it to the store where you purchased it. You will get a full refund.

If you have any questions, please call customer service at 1-800-555-1286.

What type of goods does Dawn Ltd. produce?
   (A) Audio devices
   (B) Automobiles
   (C) Electric lights
   (D) Streetlights

Let's Try!   通知文を読んで、質問に答えましょう。   CheckLink

Questions 1-2 refer to the following notice.

Liu's Kitchen Appliances
56 Columbia Avenue, Calgary, Alberta T2K 3P7

Dear Customers:

We have had several reports of failure regarding our microwave AW-1430, which has been on the market since March. Although there have been no reports of any injuries, there is the potential danger of an explosion. As a precautionary measure, we are recalling the product.

If you have purchased this model of microwave, please bring or ship it to us with proof of purchase. We will refund the purchase price within three weeks.

Your safety is our priority. If you have any questions, please e-mail us at inquiry@liukitchen.com.

Sincerely,

Ben Hogan

Ben Hogan
Manager
Customer Service Department

Notes   appliance（器具）explosion（爆発）

1. What is indicated about the microwave?
   (A) It has already caused a lot of injuries.
   (B) It sold out very quickly.
   (C) It is user-friendly.
   (D) It seems to have some serious defects.

2. What does Mr. Hogan ask customers to do?
   (A) Inquire about delivery
   (B) Make a phone call
   (C) Return a defective product for a refund
   (D) Click on the link

Grammar Tips 関係詞

関係詞のうち、ここでは**関係代名詞**について説明します。関係代名詞は、2つの文をつなぐ接続詞の役割をします。また、その直前にある名詞（先行詞）を修飾します。

I met a man.

He lives next door to us.

> I met a man **who** lives next door to us.
> 　　先行詞　　　　　　関係詞節
> （私は隣に住んでいる男性に会いました）

先行詞が人であるか物であるかによって、後ろにくる関係代名詞が変わります。

先行詞	主格	所有格	目的格
人	who	whose	who/whom
物	which	whose	which
人／物	that		that

■**主格**（who/which/that）……動詞が後ろに続く。
　The taxi driver **who** drove me to the station was really kind.
　（私を駅まで乗せてくれたタクシー運転手はとても親切でした）

■**所有格**（whose）……名詞が後ろに続く。
　Companies **whose** services are available online have gained more customers.
　（オンラインでサービスを提供している会社は、より多くの顧客を獲得しています）

■**目的格**（who/whom/which/that）……〈関係代名詞＋主語＋動詞〉の形をとる。
　The book **which** Mr. Midways ordered will be shipped soon.
　（Midways氏が注文した本はすぐに出荷されるでしょう）

Quiz 空所に適する選択肢を選んで、英文を完成させましょう。　CheckLink

The Korean man _____ visited our office was very good at speaking Japanese.
（私達の事務所を訪れた韓国人男性は、日本語が堪能でした）

　(A) who　　(B) whose　　(C) whom　　(D) which

Part 5   Check the Grammar

 ココを
Check

関係代名詞のwhatには先行詞が含まれているので、〈**what**＋**主語**＋**動詞**〉で「～すること／もの」という意味の名詞節を作ることができます。
例：What he said was true.
　　（彼が言ったことは本当でした）

Let's Try!

空所に適する選択肢を選んで、英文を完成させましょう。   ↻CheckLink

1. The package ＿＿＿ we ordered has not been delivered yet.
  (A) which   (B) whose   (C) who   (D) what
  ▶先行詞 the package の後ろにくる関係代名詞は？

2. The female clerk ＿＿＿ was at the desk seemed to be upset.
  (A) what   (B) who   (C) which   (D) whose
  ▶先行詞は人。空所の後ろには動詞が続いている。

3. ＿＿＿ Mr. Gless mentioned yesterday seemed to be sensible.
  (A) Which   (B) Whose   (C) What   (D) Who
  ▶「～したこと」という意味を表す関係代名詞は？

4. The secretary ＿＿＿ our boss recently hired is a hard worker.
  (A) which   (B) what   (C) whose   (D) whom
  ▶関係代名詞を挿入すべき空所の後ろにあるのは？

5. Brown Foods, ＿＿＿ is one of the oldest companies in San Francisco, has been quite successful.
  (A) whose   (B) who   (C) which   (D) what
  ▶先行詞は会社名。空所の後ろには動詞が続いている。

Part 1 Look at the Pictures

ココを
Check

物が主な被写体となっている写真では、その状態を一番適切に表している選択肢を選びましょう。特に、写真が撮影されている場所や物の位置関係を正確に聞き取ることが必要です。

Warm Up

CheckLink　DL 60　CD2-36　CD2-37

音声を聞いて、適切な語を空所に記入しましょう。また、(A)(B)のうち、写真の内容を正しく描写している選択肢を選びましょう。

(A) The boxes (**a**　　　) (**s**　　　　) (**u**　　　) on the trailer.

(B) The boxes (**a**　　) (**n**　　　　) (**t**　　) the trailer.

Let's Try!

CheckLink　DL 61　CD2-38

音声を聞いて、写真の内容を正しく描写している選択肢を選びましょう。

(A)　(B)　(C)　(D)

▶物の位置関係は？

Part 2   Listen to the Questions

 **ココを
Check**   Part 2には**付加疑問文**もよく出題されます。付加疑問文はYou are ~, aren't you?のように最初が肯定文なら最後を否定文にします。またYou haven't ~, have you?のように最初が否定文なら最後を肯定文にします。これらは**相手に対して軽く同意や確認を求める**ときに用いられます。

Warm Up

 CheckLink   DL 62   CD2-39 ~ CD2-42

音声を聞いて、適切な語を空所に記入しましょう。また、(A)(B)(C)のうち、質問の応答として適切な選択肢を選びましょう。

You (¹.   ) received the invoice, (².   ) you?

(A) Yes, she has been (³.   ).

(B) Not (⁴.   ).

(C) Yes, he was (⁵.   ).

Let's Try!

CheckLink   DL 63~65   CD2-43 ~ CD2-45

音声を聞いて、質問の応答として適切な選択肢を選びましょう。

1. (A) (B) (C)   ▶似ている言葉に注意しよう。

2. (A) (B) (C)   ▶「工場長」に関して、何が問われているのか注意しよう。

3. (A) (B) (C)   ▶「コピー機」をどうするのか。

Part 7 Read the Documents

 ココを Check
Part 7のMultiple Passagesには3つの文書に関する問題も出題されます。この章では、注文書が添付されている苦情文とそれに対する謝罪文を読んでみましょう。

Warm Up
2つのEメールと注文書を読んで、質問に答えましょう。

⟳ CheckLink

From:	sedgwick23@apmail.com
To:	customerservice@jungle.com
Date:	September 10
Subject:	My Order #859

———個人名がわからない担当者や関係各位に対して使う

To whom it may concern,

On August 30, I ordered *How to Succeed Efficiently* by e-mail. According to your advertisement, the DVD would be sent to my office within a few days; however, it has not been delivered yet. I telephoned customer service on September 5 and one of your staff members told me that it would arrive soon.

注文した商品の問題点についての説明

I intended to use the DVD for training new employees, but unfortunately I have not received it yet. If I do not hear from you by e-mail within two days, I will cancel the order.

———Eメールの送信者は、相手に何を要求しているのだろうか？
Please contact me at your earliest convenience.

Sincerely,

John Sedgwick
Assistant Personnel Manager
River Ltd.

Order Form (Order Number #859)

注文したのはいつ？

Name: John Sedgwick   **Date:** August 30
Address: 330 Pine Street, Seattle, Washington 98122
E-mail: sedgwick23@apmail.com

Item Description	Quantity	Price
How to Succeed Efficiently (DVD)	1	$60.00
	Shipping	Free
	TOTAL	**$60.00**

注文商品の詳細や送料の有無にも注目！

From: steve09@jungle.com
To: sedgwick23@apmail.com
Date: September 11
Subject: Order #859

1つ目のEメールへの返信だということがここでわかる

Dear Mr. Sedgwick,

Please accept our sincere apologies for your order not arriving on time.

最初に、謝罪のことばが述べられている

苦情に対する対処法は？

We will send the DVD immediately. We are also giving you a 20% discount on it. A refund will be made to your credit card.

If you have any further comments regarding this matter, please e-mail us.

Sincerely,

Steve Harston
Sales Manager

1. What is the purpose of the first e-mail?
   (A) To approve a change in policy
   (B) To enroll in a training course
   (C) To inform the company about an undelivered product
   (D) To request a refund form

2. How much is the discount that Mr. Sedgwick will get?
   (A) $48.00   (B) $20.00   (C) $13.60   (D) $12.00

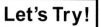
Questions 1-5 refer to the following e-mails and form.

From: tom74@yagoo.com
To: customerservice@topeye.com
Date: July 15
Subject: My Order #210

To whom it may concern,

I am writing to complain about the Polarized UV 400 Men's Sunglasses which I ordered ten days ago at the Grand Front Department Store. At that time, they were out of stock, so I placed an order. The salesclerk contacted the factory manager to inquire if my order could be shipped to me directly from the factory. Attached is a copy of my order form.

When I received the package and took out the sunglasses, one of the lenses fell out. As the sunglasses were never used, I would like to request that you issue a refund of the product price and shipping fee as soon as possible.

Please contact me at your earliest convenience.

Yours truly,

Thomas Jones

TopEye Sunglasses

Order Form

Name: Thomas Jones
Address: 24 Albert Street, Ottawa, Ontario 64214
E-mail: tom74@yagoo.com

Date: July 5
Order Number: #210

Item Description	Quantity		Price
Polarized UV 400 Men's Sunglasses	1		$55.00
		Subtotal	$55.00
		Shipping	$5.00
		TOTAL	**$60.00**

From: henry87@topeye.com
To: tom74@yagoo.com
Date: July 16
Subject: Order #210

Dear Mr. Jones,

Thank you for your inquiry. We are very sorry for the defective product.

We will refund the purchase price and the shipping fee. We will also send you a coupon. You will be able to use the coupon in any of our retail stores in Canada. Recently, we have opened stores in over 30 new cities. We are having a summer half-price sale from July 20 to August 10, so hopefully you can take advantage of this opportunity.

We hope you will accept our sincere apologies.

Best regards,

Henry Murret
Customer Support Representative
TopEye Sunglasses

1. What is the purpose of the first e-mail?
   (A) To inquire about advertised products
   (B) To ship the order
   (C) To report a product failure
   (D) To write a product review

2. When did Mr. Jones purchase the product?
   (A) July 5   (B) July 15   (C) July 16   (D) July 20

3. How much money should Mr. Jones receive?
   (A) $5   (B) $50   (C) $55   (D) $60

4. In addition to a refund, what will Mr. Jones receive from TopEye Sunglasses?
   (A) A replacement
   (B) Complimentary sunglasses
   (C) A coupon
   (D) A catalogue

5. What is true about TopEye Sunglasses?
   (A) It only offers online shopping.
   (B) It has just expanded into new areas.
   (C) It sells various types of goods, such as clothes and accessories.
   (D) It offers unique on-site customer support services.

Grammar Tips　接続詞・前置詞

接続詞は、語と語や文と文を結びつける働きをします。

■**等位接続詞**：and、but、or、soなど
対等の関係にある句や節（主語＋動詞）を結びつける。

The office was clean <u>and</u> comfortable.（事務所は清潔で快適でした）
The office seemed empty, <u>but</u> Mr. Cook was revising his sales report alone.
（事務所には誰もいないように見えましたが、Cook氏が独りで営業報告書を修正していました）

■**従位接続詞**：that、if、although/though、as soon as、because、unless、
　　　　　　　　until、when、whileなど
主節と従属節を結びつける。名詞節を作るものと副詞節を作るものがある。

We learned <u>that</u> the president had been dismissed.［名詞節］
（社長が解雇されたことを我々は知りました）

We were very happy <u>because</u> the project was successful.［副詞節］
（プロジェクトがうまくいったので、我々は非常に喜びました）

前置詞は、名詞の前に置かれて時間、場所、目的、手段、状況などを表します。

■above、at、below、by、during、from、for、in、on、over、since、to、
underなど

The bookstore opens <u>at</u> 9 A.M. <u>on</u> Sundays.
（毎週日曜日、本屋は午前9時に開店します）

There are a lot of boxes <u>in</u> the room.（部屋にたくさんの箱があります）
We go <u>to</u> the station <u>by</u> bus.（我々は駅へバスで行きます）

Quiz 空所に適する選択肢を選んで、英文を完成させましょう。　　　ＣCheckLink

Most businesspeople work either in the office _____ at home.
（ほとんどの会社員はオフィスか在宅で働きます）

　　(A) and　　　(B) nor　　　(C) or　　　(D) well

Part 6   Check the Grammar

ココを
Check

空所に前置詞と接続詞のどちらを入れるべきかを見分けることは重要です。空所の**後ろ**に**名詞（句）**があれば**前置詞**、**節（主語＋動詞）**があれば**接続詞**が必要です。また、文脈から判断して、適切な一文を選択する問題もあります。

Let's Try!   空所に適する選択肢を選んで、英文を完成させましょう。   **C**heckLink

Questions 1-4 refer to the following e-mail.

To:	Greg Stem <gstem@rmail.com>
From:	Sam Root <sam@greenet.com>
Date:	May 7
Subject:	Robson Street Studio Apartment Inquiry

I found your housing ad in today's *Global News*. ---**1.**--- June 5, I will need a new apartment. I would like to rent the studio apartment on Robson Street. ---**2.**--- it's a little far from public transportation, I am very interested in renting the place. ---**3.**---.

I look forward to hearing ---**4.**--- you soon.

Best regards,
Sam Root

1. (A) According to   (B) As of   (C) In addition to   (D) Instead of
    ▶日付けを表す表現は？

2. (A) Although   (B) If   (C) Despite   (D) When
    ▶空所の後ろには句があるか節があるか。文の意味も考えてみよう。

3. (A) Please let me know if there is anything I can do for you.
    (B) I appreciate your interest.
    (C) There is no necessary information.
    (D) Please let me know when you are available to show me the place.
    ▶前の文から「アパートに興味を持っている」ことがわかる。よって、適切な文は何か考えてみよう。

4. (A) at   (B) by   (C) from   (D) of
    ▶「連絡を待っている」という意味にするには？

Part 1 Look at the Pictures

ココを
Check
2人以上の人物が写っている写真の場合、**全員に共通する行為**に注目しましょう。
Part 1ではあまり複雑な表現は用いられませんので、人物の行為を簡潔に表現する練習を日頃から行うとよいでしょう。

Warm Up

CheckLink   DL 66   CD2-46   CD2-47

音声を聞いて、適切な語を空所に記入しましょう。また、(A)(B)のうち、写真の内容を正しく描写している選択肢を選びましょう。

(A) Women (**a**   ) (**r**   ) the
    (**d**   ) at the counter.

(B) Women (**a**   ) (**s**   )
    hands with each other.

Let's Try!

CheckLink   DL 67   CD2-48

音声を聞いて、写真の内容を正しく描写している選択肢を選びましょう。

(A)   (B)   (C)   (D)
▶3人に共通する行為は？

Part 3　Listen to the Conversations

ココを
Check

Part 3では、発話された語句がそのまま使われている選択肢もありますが、別の表現に置き換えられていることも多々あります。**キーワードとなる単語を聞き逃さないことが重要です。**

Warm Up

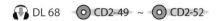

DL 68　　CD2-49　〜　CD2-52

音声を聞いて、会話の空所に適切な語を記入しましょう。

> **M:** Hello, I'd like to (1.　　　　　　) a car for next week. I'm meeting some clients in New York City, so I'd like to <u>pick it up</u> at John F. Kennedy International Airport. Are there any (2.　　　　　　) available from next Tuesday to next Saturday?
>
> **W:** Well, we only have a Japanese station wagon, a Tonda Air, next week.
>
> **M:** No problem. I've been driving that type of car for years, so I'm (3.　　　　　　) with it.
>
> **W:** That's good. Please (4.　　　　　　) out this form and show me your (5.　　　　　　).

会話中の下線部の語句の意味を選びましょう。

CheckLink

(A) 習得する　　(B) 乗せる　　(C) 受け取る　　(D) 拾い上げる

81

Warm Upの会話をもう一度聞いて、質問に答えましょう。

1. What is the man talking about?
   (A) Selling a station wagon
   (B) Renting a car
   (C) Reviewing the application form
   (D) Obtaining driving skills
   ▶男性の冒頭の発言に注意！

2. Who most likely is the woman?
   (A) A bank teller
   (B) A police officer
   (C) A clerk
   (D) A taxi driver
   ▶女性が男性に説明している内容から判断できる。

3. What does the woman ask the man to do?
   (A) E-mail her
   (B) Give her cash
   (C) Show her his identification
   (D) Visit his clients
   ▶女性の発言の最後に注意！

Part 7   Read the Documents

ココを
Check

Part 7では、新聞・雑誌の購読や会員登録などの**申込書**に関する文書も出題されます。**契約期間や料金など、具体的な内容**について読み取ることが大切です。

Warm Up   申込書を読んで、質問に答えましょう。   CheckLink

Subscription for *The Biology* magazine

———何のための申込書だろうか？

This is the application form to receive 12 monthly issues of *The Biology* magazine. We have a special discount during September. The total price is only $100. Make sure to fill in all mandatory(*) items.

Name*	First name / Last name Robert Baker
Affiliation	Student
E-mail address*	rbaker@emsg.com
E-mail confirmation*	rbaker@emsg.com
Mailing address*	2 Bell Street, Brown Plains, NY 10606
Telephone number	666-555-5678

入力されている情報をしっかり確認すること！

Payment Information

We only take credit cards.

欄外の注意事項も見落とさずに確認しよう

Credit card holder*	ROBERT BAKER
Credit card number*	2453034523457609
Expiration date*	Month / Year 04 / 24

Submit Order   Cancel

What is the purpose of the form?

(A) To subscribe magazines

(B) To download software

(C) To write an article

(D) To inquire about goods

Questions 1-2 refer to the following form.

Regent Real Estate Agency

Date: May 29

This is the lease for Apartment No. 103, located at 28 Queen Street, Lowell, Massachusetts.

Landlord: George Littlewoods
Address: 58 Bay Street, Lowell, MA 01850
Telephone: (978) 555-2234

Tenant: Edward Concord
Address: 32 Forest Street, Lowell, MA 01850
Telephone: (978) 555-1111

- By the end of every month, the tenant must pay $1,200 as the rent for the following month.
- The tenant must make all arrangements for utilities and pay for telephone, gas, electricity, water, and sewer services.

The term of this lease begins July 1. To terminate the lease, the tenant must give the landlord one month's notice.

Landlord's signature: *George Littlewoods*
Tenant's signature: *Edward Concord*

Notes ▸ lease（賃貸） sewer（下水） terminate（〜を終わらせる）

1. Who most likely made the form?
   (A) A real estate agent   (C) A building owner
   (B) Mr. Littlewoods   (D) Mr. Concord

2. What is the main purpose of the form?
   (A) To locate new housing information   (C) To state the terms of a lease
   (B) To pay telephone bills   (D) To open a bank account

Unit **13** Business

Grammar Tips 比較

原級、比較級、最上級を使って、さまざまな比較の表現をすることができます。

原級 〈as＋形容詞・副詞＋as〉	「AはBと同じくらい〜である」
	This picture is <u>as beautiful as</u> that one. （この写真はあの写真と同じくらい美しいです）
比較級 〈形容詞・副詞 -er〉 〈more＋形容詞・副詞〉	「AはBより〜である」
	Mr. Murphy works <u>harder than</u> his boss. （Murphy 氏は彼の上司よりもよく働きます）
最上級 〈the＋形容詞・副詞 -est〉 〈the most＋形容詞・副詞〉	「Aは最も〜である」（集団の中で1人・1つを他と比べる場合）
	Mr. Murphy is <u>the most experienced</u> in his department. （Murphy 氏は彼の部署の中で最も経験豊富です）

比較を表す構文には以下のようなものもあります。

■〈倍数詞＋ [as 〜 as / -er than] ...〉「…の○○倍〜な」
This package is <u>three times as heavy as</u> that one.
This package is <u>three times heavier than</u> that one.
（この小包はあの小包の3倍の重さです）

■〈The ＋比較級, the ＋比較級〉「〜すればするほど、より〜である」
<u>The busier</u> we are, <u>the harder</u> we have to work.
（忙しくなればなるほど、より一生懸命働かなければなりません）

■〈the ＋序数詞＋最上級〉「○○番目に〜な」
This is <u>the second largest</u> island in Australia.
（これはオーストラリアで2番目に大きな島です）

Quiz 空所に適する選択肢を選んで、英文を完成させましょう。　　　　**⟳**CheckLink

The clerk is the _____ in the shop. （その店員は店で一番人気があります）

  (A) more popular   (B) as popular   (C) most popular   (D) popular

Part 5 Check the Grammar

比較級・最上級の中には、**形容詞や副詞に-er/-estやmore、the mostをつけずに不規則に変化するもの**もあります。
例：good/well – better – best、bad/badly – worse – worstなど

Let's Try!

空所に適する選択肢を選んで、英文を完成させましょう。　　🗘CheckLink

1. Organic foods are _____ than processed foods.
   (A) the more healthier
   (C) healthier
   (B) healthy
   (D) healthiest
   ▶比較級の形は？

2. This country is _____ as large as that one.
   (A) three times
   (C) three
   (B) the most three
   (D) more three times
   ▶「3倍の大きさ」という意味にするには？

3. The more experienced we become, the _____ we do our jobs.
   (A) better　　(B) best　　(C) good　　(D) well
   ▶「～すればするほど、ますます…」という意味を表すのは？

4. The _____ thing of all is that no customers have visited the shop so far.
   (A) worse　　(B) worst　　(C) bad　　(D) most
   ▶空所の後ろのof allに注意しよう。

5. That tower is the _____ tallest building in the world.
   (A) two　　(B) second　　(C) most two　　(D) most second
   ▶「2番目に高い」という意味を表すのは？

Part 1 Look at the Pictures

 ココを Check 人の動作と物の状態の両方が含まれる写真では、写真を見た瞬間に人だけに注目してしまいがちです。しかし、**物の状態を描写する選択肢が正解の場合もある**ので、注意が必要です。写真全体をよく見るように心がけましょう。

Warm Up

CheckLink DL 71 CD2-58 CD2-59

音声を聞いて、適切な語を空所に記入しましょう。また、(A)(B)のうち、写真の内容を正しく描写している選択肢を選びましょう。

(A) There are several (**c**　　　　) in the
　　(**l**　　　　).

(B) People are (**f**　　　　) each (**o**　　　　).

Let's Try!

CheckLink DL 72 CD2-60

音声を聞いて、写真の内容を正しく描写している選択肢を選びましょう。

(A)　(B)　(C)　(D)

▶人の動作と物の状態は？

ココを
Check
Part 4で出題される説明文の中には、**会議やイベント、社内放送のアナウンス**などもあります。**誰が、どのような目的で話しているのか**を理解することが大切です。

Warm Up

🎧 DL 73   ◎ CD2-61 ～ ◎ CD2-63

音声を聞いて、アナウンスの空所に適切な語を記入しましょう。

Good afternoon. This is Barbara Anderson, the assistant manager of the public relations department. Today we were (1.   ) to have the business training seminar for (2.   ) in Room 103 at 4 P.M. However, as there have been electrical problems in the room since this morning, we'd like to (3.   ) you that the schedule has been changed. Participants are required to go to Room 423 at 5 P.M. Please make sure to go to the (4.   ) place on time. Before you attend the seminar, we ask that you <u>go over</u> the (5.   ) you've received. Thank you for your attention to this change.

アナウンス中の下線部の語句の意味を選びましょう。

🄲 CheckLink

(A) 〜を越える　　(B) 〜を掃除する　　(C) 〜を読み返す　　(D) 〜を視察する

Let's Try! ⟲CheckLink 🎧 DL 74 🎧 DL 75 ◎ CD2-64 ～ ◎ CD2-66 ◎ CD2-67

Warm Upのアナウンスをもう一度聞いて、質問に答えましょう。

1. Who is the speaker?
   (A) A new employee
   (B) The business instructor
   (C) An assistant manager
   (D) The president of the company
   ▷アナウンスの冒頭の言葉に注意！

2. What has been changed?
   (A) The schedule
   (B) The number of participants
   (C) The content of the seminar
   (D) The sponsor of the seminar
   ▷アナウンスで時間について述べられていることに注意しよう。

3. What does the speaker ask trainees to do?
   (A) Confirm the registration
   (B) Read the seminar information
   (C) Go to the public relations department
   (D) E-mail Ms. Anderson
   ▷話者の終盤の言葉に注意しよう。

ココを
Check

Part 7にはスケジュール表を含む通知文もよく出題されます。わかりやすくリスト化されている日程や時間など、重要なポイントを迅速に読み取るようにしましょう。

Warm Up 通知文を読んで、質問に答えましょう。 ♪CheckLink

NBTC
Intensive Computer Training Classes

The National Business Training Center will offer the following intensive computer training classes:

Class	Date	Time	Cost
Word	June 24–26	9:30 A.M.–11:30 A.M.	$30
Excel	June 27–29	1:00 P.M.–3:00 P.M.	$35
PowerPoint	June 28–30	4:00 P.M.–6:00 P.M.	$40

各クラスの日程や時間がわかりやすく示されている

Classes will be held at Houston Business Junior College, 92 Space Road, Colonel City. If you would like to register for them, please e-mail Vincent Kwon, course coordinator, at vkwon@nationalbusiness.ac. Registration will begin on June 1.

開催場所や登録方法についての情報もしっかり把握しよう!

What is the subject of the notice?

(A) Regulations of a business school
(B) Information about computer classes
(C) Registration for exercise classes
(D) Advertisement for new computers

Let's Try!

通知文を読んで、質問に答えましょう。

Questions 1-2 refer to the following notice.

The 5th Asian Business Workshop

Dear Colleagues,

On August 1, the 5th Asian Business Workshop will be held in Room 241 of the Osaka Library. We will have three presentations. The schedule is as follows:

Presenter	Theme	Time
Taro Doi	Business Research Methods in East Asia	1:00 P.M. – 2:00 P.M.
Julia Nakanishi	Business Cycles in Japan	2:15 P.M. – 3:15 P.M.
Gordon Fujita	Business Models for Automobile Markets	3:30 P.M. – 4:30 P.M.

You will have the chance to meet experts in various fields. Refreshments will be served after the last session.

For further information, visit http://www.asianbusiness.jp or contact me at sato@gnet.com.

Yoshio Sato
Sales Manager

Notes method（方法） refreshments（軽食）

1. Who will give the final presentation?
   (A) Taro Doi   (C) Gordon Fujita
   (B) Julia Nakanishi (D) Yoshio Sato

2. The word "session" in paragraph 2, line 2, is closest in meaning to
   (A) advertisement   (C) industry
   (B) design   (D) period

Grammar Tips 仮定法

仮定法は、「事実と異なる」ことを表すときに使います。仮定法の文中では、動詞や助動詞が現実の「時」とずれるのが特徴です。

■仮定法過去·········現在の事実に反する仮定を表す。

〈If＋主語＋[動詞の過去形/were], 主語＋[would/should/could/might]＋動詞の原形〉「もし～なら、…でしょう」

If I <u>were</u> you, I <u>would do</u> my best. (もし私があなたなら、全力を尽くすでしょう)

■仮定法過去完了·········過去の事実に反する仮定を表す。

〈If＋主語＋had＋過去分詞, 主語＋[would/should/could/might]＋have＋過去分詞〉「もし～だったら、…だったでしょう」

If the patient <u>had known</u> Dr. Davis, she <u>would have seen</u> him then.
(もしその患者がDavis医師を知っていたなら、その時、彼の診察を受けていたでしょう)

■仮定法過去完了＋仮定法過去·········過去の事実に反する仮定に対して、現在の事実に反することを述べる。

〈If＋主語＋had＋過去分詞, 主語＋[would/should/could/might]＋動詞の原形〉「もし～だったら、…でしょう」

If the patient <u>had taken</u> medicine, he <u>would feel</u> better now.
(もしその患者が薬を服用していたなら、今頃は良くなっているでしょう)

Quiz 空所に適する選択肢を選んで、英文を完成させましょう。 **⟳CheckLink**

If we _____ together, we could launch a new project.
(もし我々が一緒なら、新しいプロジェクトを始められるでしょう)

(A) is   (B) was   (C) were   (D) have

Part 5 Check the Grammar

ココを
Check
要求・提案・勧告・主張・必要・願望などの意味を表す動詞や形容詞に続く **that 節中の動詞は原形**となります。

例：The doctor advised that Mr. Burns take medicine.
（Burns 氏が薬を服用するよう医師はアドバイスをしました）

この他にも、demand、desirable、essential、imperative、important、insist、necessary、recommend、request、suggest などがこの例に当てはまります。

Let's Try!

空所に適する選択肢を選んで、英文を完成させましょう。　　　　　　　　　　 ↻ CheckLink

1. If Ms. Lewis had not broken her leg, she _____ New York.
   (A) would　　(B) would have visited　　(C) visited　　(D) had visited
   ▶仮定法過去完了を表すのは？

2. If the assistant _____ tired, she would work overtime.
   (A) is　　(B) was　　(C) were　　(D) were not
   ▶仮定法過去で、文脈に適切なのは？

3. It is desirable that inpatients _____ to their rooms after their friends and family visit them.
   (A) return　　(B) had returned　　(C) returned　　(D) had been returning
   ▶that 節の前に desirable があることに注意しよう。

4. If we had not called an ambulance, the baby _____ be in a coma now.
   (A) had　　(B) will　　(C) may　　(D) might
   ▶文末の now に注目しよう。

5. Health experts insisted that we _____ a medical checkup at least once a year.
   (A) had　　(B) have　　(C) had had　　(D) have had
   ▶that 節の前の insisted に注意しよう。

Part 1 Look at the Pictures

ココを
Check

この章では、**乗り物が被写体となっている写真**について学習します。まず、vehicle（乗り物）、truck（トラック）、motorcycle（バイク）、bicycle/bike（自転車）などの名称を覚えておきましょう。音声を聞く前に、乗り物がどのような状態で写っているのか確認することも大切です。

Warm Up

ⓒ CheckLink 🎧 DL 76 ◎ CD2-68 ◎ CD2-69

音声を聞いて、適切な語を空所に記入しましょう。また、(A)(B) のうち、写真の内容を正しく描写している選択肢を選びましょう。

(A) A vehicle (i   ) (m   ) on the (h   ).

(B) A vehicle (i   ) (p   ) under the building.

Let's Try!

ⓒ CheckLink 🎧 DL 77 ◎ CD2-70

音声を聞いて、写真の内容を正しく描写している選択肢を選びましょう。

(A) (B) (C) (D)

▶乗り物の種類と状態を確認しよう。

Part 2 Listen to the Questions

ココを
Check
Part 2の問題は、疑問文ではなく**平叙文で始まる**こともあります。その場合、**相手に何かを伝えたいという意図を表している**ことが多いと言えます。全文をしっかり聞き取って、発話内容を正確に把握しましょう。

Warm Up

CheckLink   DL 78   CD2-71 ~ CD2-74

音声を聞いて、適切な語を空所に記入しましょう。また、(A)(B)(C) のうち、質問の応答として適切な選択肢を選びましょう。

I'm not (1.   )
(2.   ) today.

(A) I have an appointment
   with the (3.   ).

(B) You did a good
   (4.   ).

(C) Why don't you
   go to the
   (5.   )
   on your way
   home?

Let's Try!

CheckLink   DL 79~81   CD2-75 ~ CD2-77

音声を聞いて、質問の応答として適切な選択肢を選びましょう。

1.　(A)　(B)　(C)　▶話者の要望に適切に答えている選択肢を選ぼう。
2.　(A)　(B)　(C)　▶話し手はどうしてがっかりしたのだろうか。
3.　(A)　(B)　(C)　▶何が問題となっているのか。

Part 7 Read the Documents

ココを
Check

8章と11章に続き、14章でもMultiple Passagesの問題を学習します。ここでは、医療に関連した求人広告とそれに対する問い合わせのEメールを読んでみましょう。

Warm Up | 求人広告とEメールを読んで、質問に答えましょう。　　　○CheckLink

Nurses Needed

————職場と仕事の概要は？

Hakata Christian Hospital is seeking dedicated and responsible nurses at the rehabilitation facility, which will be further renovated again in August.

Candidates must have at least three years' experience in a similar role. In addition, as the number of non-Japanese residents has increased in this region, a command of other languages besides Japanese is required. Candidates with a nursing vocational school certificate are eligible.

> 応募条件について説明されている

Hours will be 8:00 A.M. to 4:00 P.M., 4:00 P.M. to 12:00 A.M., or 12:00 A.M. to 8:00 A.M., five days a week, working in shifts. A competitive salary will be provided.

> 勤務内容や待遇について説明されている

If you are interested in applying, please e-mail Midori Yamada at myamada@hakata-health.or.jp.

Please attach your résumé with a cover letter no later than June 20.

> 必要書類の種類と締め切り日は？

96

From: carla@acb.ne.jp

To: myamada@hakata-health.or.jp

Date: June 1

Subject: Nursing position

Dear Ms. Yamada,

―――1つ目の文書への返信だということがわかる

I am writing in response to your advertisement on the website. I was excited to hear about the position. Since graduating from the National Nursing University in Osaka, I have been working at the University Hospital for five years.

I have mainly been working with inpatients. Specifically, since I am helping surgeons, my role has been taking care of patients before surgeries and then working with them in rehabilitation until they leave the hospital.

I am enthusiastic about my current job, but unfortunately, my hospital will be downsizing because of financial problems.

経歴の紹介や自己アピール

I am confident that I am an ideal candidate for this job. In addition, I am originally from the United States and have been living in Japan for 20 years. I am bilingual in English and Japanese.

Attached is my résumé with a cover letter. I look forward to hearing from you. ―――添付物が明記されている

Yours faithfully,

Carla Morimoto

1. What kind of position is being advertised?
   (A) Accountant　　(B) Midwife　　(C) Nurse　　(D) Pharmacist

2. What is true about Ms. Morimoto?
   (A) She meets the job requirements.　　(C) She was born in Japan.
   (B) She just graduated from university.　　(D) She is 20 years old.

Questions 1-5 refer to the following advertisement and e-mail.

Volunteers Needed for Clinical Trials

Ocean Clinical Trial Center in Guam is looking for volunteers to test our medicines before they are sold on the market. Ocean Clinical Trial Center was founded for the purpose of making effective medicine which can prevent and cure diseases.

Volunteer opportunities include participating in trials and helping in the office. Nursing students may be able to assist with our clinical trials. Hours are flexible. Volunteers must be at least 18 years of age and have their own transportation.

If you are interested in volunteer details, please e-mail Amy Lee, Volunteer Coordinator, at ocean@ne.ac.

Note flexible（融通のきく）

From:	pacific@zmal.cs
To:	ocean@ne.ac
Date:	May 10
Subject:	Volunteering

Dear Ms. Lee,

I am interested in your advertisement. I am a nursing student and would like to volunteer to help with clinical trials. It will be useful for me to understand more about medicine.

I am attaching my résumé, which includes the nursing courses I have taken. It would be great if you could let me know about the details of the work I could do for the clinical trials. My summer vacation begins on May 24, so I will be able to volunteer at the center anytime after that.

I look forward to hearing from you.

Sincerely,

Joan Royce

1. What is the purpose of the advertisement?
   (A) To sell medication
   (B) To call for volunteers
   (C) To renovate nursing homes
   (D) To warn about epidemics

2. In the advertisement, the word "founded" in paragraph 1, line 3, is closest in meaning to
   (A) confirmed   (B) established   (C) demolished   (D) discovered

3. Why did Ms. Royce send the e-mail?
   (A) To apply for a part-time job
   (B) To reply to the e-mail
   (C) To ask about volunteer work
   (D) To visit her friends

4. Who is Ms. Royce?
   (A) A student   (B) A nurse   (C) A doctor   (D) A recruiter

5. What will Ms. Royce most likely NOT do as a volunteer?
   (A) Assist with the trials
   (B) Help with office work
   (C) Participate in the trials
   (D) Transport medicines

Part 1

CCheckLink **DL 82, 83** ⊙ CD2-78 ⊙ CD2-79

Look at the picture and choose the statement that best describes what you see.

1.

(A)　(B)　(C)　(D)

2.

(A)　(B)　(C)　(D)

Part 2

CCheckLink **DL 84~87** ⊙ CD2-80 ~ ⊙ CD2-83

Listen to the question and the three responses, and choose the best response to each question.

3.　(A)　(B)　(C)
4.　(A)　(B)　(C)
5.　(A)　(B)　(C)
6.　(A)　(B)　(C)

Part 3

 CheckLink DL 88 DL 89  CD2-84 ~ CD2-90 CD2-91

Listen to the conversation and choose the best answer to each question.

Extension Numbers

0	Front desk
5	Cleaning service
8	Café and restaurant service
10	Tour desk counter
*9	Local call
*011	International call

7. Where most likely are the speakers?
   (A) At a jazz bar
   (B) At a hotel
   (C) At a restaurant
   (D) At a ticket counter

8. Why did the woman make a phone call?
   (A) To change her room
   (B) To extend her stay
   (C) To inquire about concert tickets
   (D) To order room service

9. Look at the graphic. Which extension number did the woman call?
   (A) Ext. 0
   (B) Ext. 5
   (C) Ext. 8
   (D) Ext. 10

Listen to the short talk and choose the best answer to each question.

10. What is the main purpose of the message?
    (A) To announce repair services
    (B) To inform customers of banking services
    (C) To negotiate contracts
    (D) To upgrade computer software

11. According to the message, what type of service is provided?
    (A) Account information
    (B) Mailing shopping catalogues
    (C) Proofreading documents
    (D) Housing services

12. What does the speaker suggest listeners do?
    (A) Go to the website
    (B) Refer to a brochure
    (C) Renew a credit card
    (D) Visit the bank anytime

Part 5

Choose the best answer to complete the sentence.

13. The guest speaker reviewed his topic _____ before he gave his speech.
    (A) intensive
    (B) intensively
    (C) intensiveness
    (D) intensify

14. We avoided _____ discussions in the meeting because most of the issues were unimportant.
    (A) having
    (B) to have
    (C) had
    (D) have

15. _____ there was no accident, the road was very crowded.
    (A) If   (B) However   (C) Since   (D) Although

16. All of the customers' data at Ikeda Sports has been _____ for decades.
    (A) confidential
    (B) impatient
    (C) sensible
    (D) rapid

17. Ms. Smith came back to the office and then talked to _____ assistant.
    (A) she   (B) they   (C) her   (D) hers

18. _____ Mr. Cheng told us yesterday turned out to be true.
    (A) Which   (B) What   (C) Whose   (D) That

19. All of our new employees _____ to join the upcoming project meeting.
    (A) are invited
    (B) invited
    (C) was invited
    (D) invite

Part 6

Questions 20-23 refer to the following article.

New York (October 3) — New York Health Food Corp. announced today that it will spend about $2 million to improve the quality of its West New York plants. The company will install new devices to manufacture ---**20.**--- more efficiently and safely. The new devices are expected to increase the company's production by at least 30 percent over the next two years. ---**21.**---, the same types of devices were installed at its East New York plants last year. Since then, the company's production has ---**22.**--- by roughly 10 percent. ---**23.**---. Consequently, several types of new products should be released late next year.

20. (A) approvals
   (B) products
   (C) improvements
   (D) outcomes

21. (A) Besides
   (B) In contrast
   (C) However
   (D) In fact

22. (A) raise
   (B) rose
   (C) raised
   (D) risen

23. (A) Spokesperson will have a press conference to explain the company's new hiring policies.
   (B) Much of the increase in profits was invested in research and development.
   (C) Innovative sales strategies didn't lead to last year's achievements.
   (D) The plant manager is likely to reduce working hours as soon as possible.

Part 7

Questions 24-25 refer to the following text-message chain.   CheckLink

---

Greg Evans (9:17 A.M.)

Hi, Annie. Did you enjoy your trip yesterday?

Annie Sato (9:19 A.M.)

Not really. My baggage was delayed last night because of the limited transfer time, so I didn't get it until 4:30 A.M.

Greg Evans (9:21 A.M.)

That's too bad. I've had problems on business trips too. When I was going to a conference in New York last winter, I had to make a transfer in Chicago. However, almost all the flights were canceled due to a snowstorm. I needed to stay overnight there.

Annie Sato (9:25 A.M.)

Oh, no, where did you spend that night?

Greg Evans (9:30 A.M.)

Luckily, they got me a hotel room. I flew out later and joined the conference the following day.

Annie Sato (9:34 A.M.)

Anyway, I'm glad I came back safely. It was very stressful, though. Next time I travel, I hope everything will be okay.

---

24. What is being discussed?

    (A) Carry-on baggage   (C) Travel problems

    (B) Cancellation of a flight   (D) Discount tickets

25. At 9:19 A.M., what does Ms. Sato most likely mean when she writes, "Not really"?

    (A) She is no longer waiting for her luggage.

    (B) She is reluctant to change her plan.

    (C) She is not interested in her business trip.

    (D) She thinks her trip was difficult.

From:	mnakamura@go-net.ne.jp
To:	paul.diem@rpahawaii.com
Date:	March 4
Subject:	Tax Accounting Assistant

Dear Mr. Diem,

I am interested in the position of tax accounting assistant advertised on your website.

I have been working for an accounting firm in Tokyo for the past five years. My tasks consist of processing tax returns, doing secretarial work, and training new employees. I also interpret at the firm's meetings with English-speaking clients.

I have enjoyed my work here, but my husband has been transferred to Hawaii, so I am looking for a position in Honolulu. I am very motivated and I am an excellent team player.

I would greatly appreciate it if you would consider my application. I have attached my résumé and references to this e-mail. If you require more information, please e-mail me at mnakamura@go-net.ne.jp.

I look forward to hearing from you.

Sincerely,

Mariko Nakamura

From: paul.diem@rpahawaii.com

To: mnakamura@go-net.ne.jp

Date: March 5

Subject: Re: Tax Accounting Assistant

Dear Ms. Nakamura,

Thank you for e-mailing me with your résumé and references. I am impressed by your career and your interest in the position.

I would like to have an online interview as soon as possible. We have a large number of Japanese clients, so a Japanese speaker would be preferable for this position. Your practical work experience will also be helpful to us.

Please let me know when you are available for the interview. I would appreciate it if we can schedule it by 4 P.M Honolulu time on a weekday.

Best regards,

Paul Diem
Personnel Manager
RPA Hawaii

---

26. What is the purpose of the first e-mail?
   (A) To apply for an advertised job
   (B) To inquire about travel information
   (C) To train new staff
   (D) To search for housing information

27. Where is the applicant now?
   (A) In Tokyo   (B) In Osaka   (C) In Honolulu   (D) In New York

28. In the second e-mail, the word "preferable" in paragraph 2, line 2, is closest in meaning to
   (A) accidental   (B) inappropriate   (C) individual   (D) desirable

29. What is the purpose of the second e-mail?

   (A) To find a Japanese teacher

   (B) To send a résumé

   (C) To ask about job details

   (D) To set up an interview

30. What is NOT indicated about Ms. Nakamura?

   (A) She is a strong candidate for the position.

   (B) She speaks both English and Japanese.

   (C) She is married.

   (D) She is from Hawaii.

本書には CD（別売）があります

NEW GATEWAY TO THE TOEIC® L&R TEST
新 イラスト・図解で学ぶ TOEIC® L&R テスト はじめの一歩

2021 年 1 月 20 日 初版第 1 刷発行
2023 年 2 月 20 日 初版第 6 刷発行

編　者	David P. Thompson
	仲　川　浩　世
	宮　野　智　靖

発行者	福　岡　正　人
発行所	株式会社 **金星堂**

（〒101-0051）東京都千代田区神田神保町 3-21
Tel.（03）3263-3828（営業部）
　　（03）3263-3997（編集部）
Fax（03）3263-0716
https://www.kinsei-do.co.jp

編集担当／西田 碧　　　　　　　　　Printed in Japan
印刷所・製本所／萩原印刷株式会社

ISBN978-4-7647-4126-3 C1082